SUFFERING AND THE CONTEMPLATIVE

The phenomenon of suffering, its nature and its purpose are issues that have long perplexed humanity. How are we to interpret and accept illness and injury? Are they signs of the wrath of God?

Drawing on his studies, his professional knowledge and a deep reading of the scriptures, Jack Baxter traces the pattern of disease from earliest times to the present day and examines humankind's parallel attempts to cure and prevent illness. He looks particularly closely at the many descriptions of illness in the Bible and shows how these afflictions provide opportunities for God to reveal his healing powers. Illness, for Jack Baxter, is a metaphor for humanity's flawed relationship with God. He associates human susceptibility to disease with man's fall from divine grace.

Jack Baxter's own experience of suffering adds a personal dimension to his arguments. Through daily contemplative prayer he strives to understand and accept pain both in himself and in others. His book will be a valuable guide to those seeking insight into the role of suffering in God's plan.

To   Horace

With every good wish

Jack Baxter.

3rd August '92.

SUFFERING AND THE CONTEMPLATIVE

Jack Baxter

JANUS PUBLISHING COMPANY
London, England

First published in Great Britain 1992 by
Janus Publishing Company

© Jack Baxter 1991

**British Library Cataloguing-in-Publication Data.
A catalogue record for this book is available from
the British Library.**

ISBN 1 85756 080 9

Cover design David Murphy

Phototypeset by Intype, London

Printed & bound in England by
Antony Rowe Ltd, Chippenham, Wiltshire

Contents

List of illustrations

Preface

Recently, while having my 'quiet' time – that time of the day which I lay aside for prayer and when I consciously try to contemplate the presence of God within me – I became aware that I was able to see the whole of my spiritual life stretched out before me as a single entity, with particular reference to suffering and the role of contemplation. Everything that I knew and believed in about God and these experiences was seen with remarkable clarity. There was nothing here which I did not understand. The whole experience was devoid of doubts. There was no thought process, yet there was profound lucidity. When the sublimity of the moment passed, I found myself thinking in modern jargon and uttering – 'I've cracked it!' Having cracked it, what then was I to do with it? I must share my experience with others, certainly. But how? I could not begin to tell by word of mouth; and of writing, my experience in the past had been nothing beyond publishing the odd paper and producing a dissertation for a post-graduate qualification at Birmingham University. Yet writing seemed to be the obvious choice. I chose the title 'Suffering and the Contemplative': suffering because it is something that most of us are familiar with, some more than others; and the contemplative part simply because the prayers of the contemplative are often the only way left when the suffering persists, when medicine and all other remedies seem to have failed.

I have tried to trace the origins of suffering through the origins of disease. Some may wonder that I found it necessary to go back hundreds of thousands, even millions of years. The answer is that I wanted to dispel all thoughts and feelings about the allegorical story of the Genesis, which, useful as it may be, only serves to condense several million years of morphological and genetic evolution. If one believes that the Garden of Eden story is an authentic account of the beginning of life and the creation of humankind, then I have no wish to damage the idea. I would say, though: have a look at the anthropological evidence, most of which is irrefutable and which gives a much clearer account of what really happened. There are some, and I suspect those of fundamentalist religious belief, who say, science and religion do not mix. I have always found this difficult to accept. God the Father is the creator of the universe with all its marvellous scientific wonders. Surely such a God must be the greatest scientist of all! As for the religious part – man was created by God, for God. Further, the features ascribed to scientific matters, and the attributes peculiar to salvation by faith in Jesus Christ, have the same common origin, namely, God the Father. So where is the problem? Both by their common origin not only identify with each other but complement each other.

Acknowledgements

I am indebted to James Borst and Joyce Huggett who by their writings have enabled me to place a label on contemplative prayer, a practice in which I have engaged for many years, and which I have always referred to as my 'quiet' time. They have helped to deepen my commitment by their wise and erudite writings and given fresh impetus to a well tried practice.

I am also indebted to James Borst for the two quotations from Pope John XXIII and St John of the Cross.

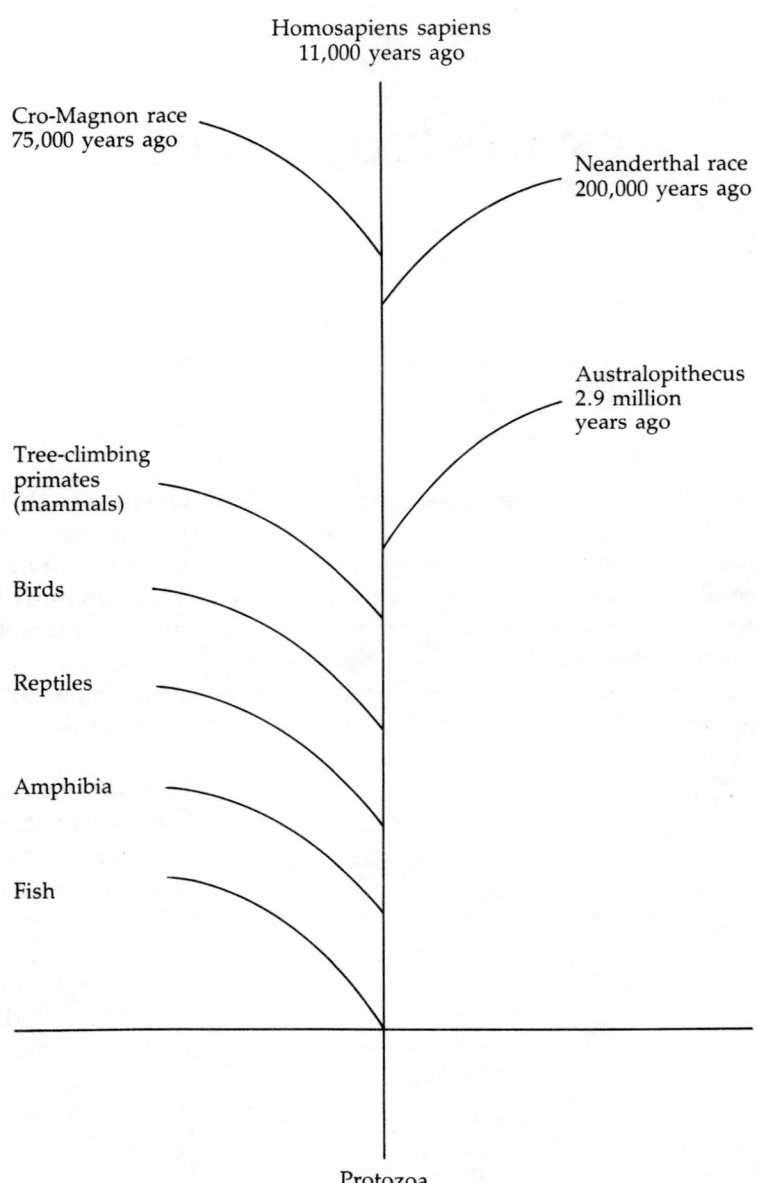

Figure 1. Diagrammatic representation of the animal kingdom showing the ascent of humankind

1

The evolution of humankind

Suffering and disease are just two of the afflictions that modern man (Homosapiens sapiens) has fallen heir to. If we are to trace the origin of these we have to go back some 200,000 years to that point where modern man began to emerge from his evolutionary forbears. Further, if we wish to test the significance of humankind's salvation with the amount of suffering it has endured then we have to try to bridge the gap between scientific proof and religious belief. This task is not an easy one for humanity has always fought shy of linking the two.

The evolution of humankind is not confined to a single species (Bronowski 1973), but is made up of several races which had their beginnings near the equator in Central Africa two million years ago. One thing, however, is apparent – modern man did not come from one particular area. Evolution does not work like this (Ross-Macdonald 1975). We are the result of considerable intermingling of different sub-species. For example, at the end of the Pleistocene Ice Age, the areas now known as Europe, Western Asia and North Africa were inhabited by the Neanderthal race (Homosapiens neanderthalensis) (Ross-MacDonald 1975). This sub-species was no more than five feet tall and was heavily built with massive jaws, thick neck and large hands (Ross-MacDonald 1975).

Bronowski (1973), however, gives good reasons why he considers that the evolutionary process was begun between Northern Kenya and Southwest Ethiopia. This evidence is further substantiated by the findings of Leakey (1981), with the discovery of a skull belonging to Australopithecus near Lake Rudolph in North Kenya. He puts the date of Australopithecus much earlier, at 2.9 million years ago.

As already mentioned, there is definite anthropological evidence dating from the end of the Pleistocene Ice Age, about 200,000 years ago, of the genus Homo in the species H. neanderthalensis (Eaton 1970). By now extreme climatic and environmental conditions had caused this forerunner to migrate north to present-day Israel (Bronowski 1973), and this by the way suggests a much more likely place for the so-called, allegorical, Garden of Eden mentioned in the Book of Genesis. Further evidence for this lies in the series of human and sub-human remains found at Mount Carmel in Israel (Ross MacDonald 1975). Current opinion, however, tends to suggest that modern Iraq is a more likely place for the Garden of Eden (Blue 1991).

The bones found at Mount Carmel have been identified as having belonged to H. neanderthalensis and another sub-species H. Cro-Magnon. Ross-MacDonald (1975) suggests that the two sub-species mentioned may well have interbred, and that approximately 75,000 years ago H. Cro-Magnon replaced H. neanderthalensis by virtue of disease resistance and inventiveness. At the same time the genus Homo continued to evolve alongside H. Cro-Magnon and it seems likely that the latter was replaced entirely by H. sapiens, even although vestiges of H. neanderthalensis still persisted. Some anthropologists believe that certain modern European populations still carry the Neanderthal genes (Ross-MacDonald 1975).

From this one can only assume that as Cro-Magnon replaced Neanderthal Man, so Homosapiens sapiens replaced Cro-Magnon at about 11,000 BC. With the origin of the species Homosapiens sapiens, the phylogenetic evolution of H. sapiens comes to an end for the time being. This would seem to be the case as far as detectable morphological change is concerned (Mazak 1980). All that we are able to reconstruct is the development of human intellect and human culture, with modern civilisation as its end product (Mazak 1980). To this I would also add the development of a spiritual nature or faculty.

Eleven thousand years ago, Malcolm Ross-MacDonald (1975) points out, the human population was small and stable. The apparent suppression of the population, he argues, was thought at one time to be due entirely to crude environmental factors, such as disease and famine similar to those found in more recent times prior to the advent of proper sanitation. He shows that the last thirty years have revealed much anthropological evidence to suggest that population size was carefully regulated, not by crude environmental factors but probably by some form of birth control. He also believes that, contrary to older beliefs, poverty, squalor, epidemics and senseless violence were not the controlling influences in population size and that these belong to more recent times. This same author believes that population size must have been regulated and controlled by cultural means. This communal response to population size seems to bear a direct relationship to the carrying capacity of the environment. Ross-MacDonald does not state what these cultural controls were, but he is quite definite that they were not hardship. He further goes on to say that for thousands of years humanity enjoyed a standard of living so high that it has not been bettered for a significant proportion of Western populations until after the Industrial Revolution.

We now have the ideal scenario for a Garden of Eden-type existence. I say 'ideal' because Homosapiens sapiens inherited the perfect climatic conditions mentioned by Bronowski (1973) when early man migrated north to Mount Carmel in modern Israel to escape the aridity of Northern Kenya and Southwest Ethiopia; although, as already mentioned, current-day thinking suggests that a site for the Garden of Eden was probably slightly east of Israel in what is now Iraq (Blue 1991). Humankind also acquired the socio–economic advantage described by Ross-MacDonald (1975), and presumably also inherited and enjoyed the disease resistance and inventiveness that caused H. Cro-Magnon to triumph over H. neanderthalensis. This latter piece of conjecture falls well within the the realms of probability in that in order for a species to survive it has to win the evolutionary struggle or become extinct. Since H. Cro-Magnon triumphed over H. neanderthalensis because of disease resistance and inventiveness it is hardly likely that Homosapiens sapiens would discard this advantage in the struggle for survival, and certainly not to begin with. This ideal situation continued for thousands of years, and was never equalled by Western civilisations until well into the eighteenth century (Ross-MacDonald 1975).

Before leaving this period one thing has become clear. Chrono-logically and historically the Eden tragedy happened at a point between 11,000 and 2,000 BC. This can be adduced because of the socio–economic advantages cited by Ross-MacDonald (1975), which he claims lasted for thousands of years. Thus it would seem that H. sapiens inherited the disease resistance enjoyed by his forbears and this must have lasted for some considerable time. Further evidence which corroborates this belief lies in the findings of the anthropological sciences which show that humanity later suffered injury, congenital abnormalities, scurvy, bone tumours, arthritis, dental diseases, tuberculosis and leprosy (Rhodes 1985). These it endured for a considerable time prior to the arrival of the Hebrew patriarchs and the tribes of Israel. This suggests that the golden era of socio–economic advantage and disease resistance came earlier rather than later in the period 11,000 to 2,000 BC. The ending of this halcyon period also suggests that some form of catastrophe overtook the human race. Evolutionwise and morpho-logically, H. sapiens had reached the peak of perfection and any further development would need to have been cultural or spiritual. From what has already been said, during this period around 11,000 BC, H. sapiens was near to achieving this. Then comes the catas-trophe. Could this be what the theologians call the Eden tragedy – the first apostasy? Whether we accept the allegorical version of the Genesis story or a more enlightened version, one thing is clear – humanity had lost its integrity, virtue and innocence and had inherited a proclivity to sin. Theologically this is referred to as the Fall. The editors of Black's Bible Dictionary (1959) state that psychologically humanity's experience in the Fall is true, and that symbolically the Genesis story is an early attempt to explain the sources of suffering, illness, disease, man's hard toil, woman's travail and her subordination to man. Be that as it may, by the year 2,000 BC, H. sapiens had more than its fair share of these.

2

The early practice of medicine in the Near East

Perhaps with hindsight humankind could have realised the importance of the adage that 'prevention is better than cure'. Because of the Eden tragedy it was to take several thousand years to pay for this mistake, and unravel the ramifications of disease and its aetiological factors. Only then did humanity grasp the significance of preventive medicine and that came after generations of suffering, observation, experimentation and much trial and error. No sooner had we faced and conquered one area of disease, when we were again faced with others, sometimes running concurrently, but often coming like a bolt out of the blue. It was as though humankind was out of step with what should have been its natural destiny. Yet, in spite of the overwhelming odds, we seem always to have the rare ability to conquer our environment. It is with these thoughts in mind that we start to trace the processes of disease and suffering and all the other implications that are co-terminous with suffering humanity.

Throughout these historical manifestations we get glimpses of God's redeeming love, guiding, prodding and revealing his healing grace. We see it in the Patriarchs and healers of the Old Testament. We see it in Christ's earthly life and in the healing miracles of the early church. We see it in the deliberations of the Greek philosophers; the Roman engineers; the Hindus with their early yet advanced surgical techniques. We see it in the dark days of the Middle Ages when all real scholarship ceased to exist, when it appeared in blinding flashes of faith and miraculous cures. Finally, we see it in the men of science from the Renaissance onwards. It is with these thoughts that we begin to unravel the mystery.

The practice of medicine in the Near East 2000 years before Christ was a curious mixture of observation and curative methods which occasionally worked, and a form of mysticism closely linked to superstition which invariably failed to work. The dominating cultures of the time belonged to the natives of Mesopotamia (now known as Iraq), the Egyptians and the ancient Hebrews from Israel. All of these had certain similarities in their attitudes to medical affairs in that they believed that the air was full of demons and evil spirits. The Mesopotamians and Egyptians believed that illness and disease struck when the individual or the nation was out of favour with the gods. The Israelites on the other hand believed in a monotheistic God who controlled the destiny of the nation as well as that of the individual; for them illness and disease were a punishment from God for sin and wrongdoing. This belief had a profound effect upon reducing the magical element in curative medicine at that time.

The Mesopotamians, although immensely superstitious, did not have the same attachment to their various gods and were quick to notice by sheer cause and effect methods, that accidents caused broken bones and other injuries. They also recognised the connection between infection and disease (Coleman 1985). It could be said that they were in some ways more responsible for putting the practice of medicine on to a scientific basis than the Israelites, whose stubbornness did much to hold up the development of medicine in a rational and scientific way.

Other contributions to the medical scene at that time came from the Egyptians. Their custom of embalming and mummifying gave them a great advantage over their contemporaries especially in the field of practical anatomy. They did not have the same scruples about the dissection of the human body.

Most inhabitants of the Near East, as already seen, had the attitude that sickness and illness were a direct result of offending against prevalent gods, or punishment from the God of Israel for sins committed. Enlightened men, like the author of the Book of Job, courageously challenged this mistaken belief, and insisted that some sufferers were undoubtedly innocent (Heaton 1956).

When illnesses and afflictions were not ascribed directly to God, they were thought by the Israelites (as well as others) to be the work of demons and evil spirits which could only be removed by various rituals and incantations; a practice which was frowned on and actively discouraged by Israel's religious leaders.

Some of the curses mentioned in the Psalms were not meant for human enemies, but were undoubtedly intended for the demons of disease. Similarly, people afflicted with strokes were thought to have been struck by some supernatural agent; and the delirium of fever was thought to be the result of demon possession. This strange mixture of fear and uncertainty undoubtedly caused the Israelites to regard lunatics with mingled pity and fear. David used this ruse to advantage before the King of Gath (1 Samuel 21:12–15), when he feigned madness (Heaton 1956).

Perhaps we have the nearest approach to a modern physician in the person of Elisha. He was familiar with leprosy (2 Kings 5:27); he knew about disinfecting water (2 Kings 2:20 ff); and about ridding food of poison (2 Kings 4:41). He also restored a dead boy to life (2 Kings 4:22–37).

Another example of Old Testament healing is found with the person of Isaiah. He was summoned by King Hezekiah who was suffering from a boil. The prophet prescribed a fig poultice which had the desired effect and the patient was healed (Isaiah 38:1–9).

Other examples of healing in the Old Testament are more of the miraculous variety. Abraham prayed to God and God healed Abimelech, his wife and their slave girls so that they could have children again (Genesis 20:17); and Moses cried out to the Lord (Numbers 12:13) so that Miriam should be healed of her leprosy.

Another example of healing, with a slight twist, occurs with Asa (2 Chronicles 16:12) 'In the thirty-ninth year [of his reign], he was crippled by a severe foot disease; but even then he did not turn to the Lord for help, but to doctors'. Records do not show what the physician prescribed for the king's gout or what his status was, but the evidence suggests that this could be an attempt by the physician to turn his professionalism to advantage and gain royal patronage, in order to acquire independence from the religious leaders of the time (Heaton 1956), and presumably achieve what we now call clinical freedom.

The Israelites could not accept that there could be anything remotely scientific about bodily functions or the diseases that affected them. Human life was a gift from God and disease and affliction the result of sin. The cure lay only in forgiveness, a closer adherence to the will of God and the ten commandments. As for studying anatomy and the associated sciences, such as physiology and pathology – the whole was anathema to the Hebrew way of thinking. To tamper with dead bodies was abhorrent and was anyway forbidden by the religious teachers of the time.

Despite these self-imposed limitations they had acquired considerable practical, although unsystematic, knowledge about disease and suffering. Priests had, for example, considerable diagnostic skills in dealing with skin afflictions such as leprosy (Leviticus 13:20). They were also well versed in matters of hygiene, and many of the rules of health were legislatively enforced. Much of their knowledge had been acquired on a trial and error basis, yet we learn of how the Philistines sacrificed five golden mice to appease heathen gods in the hope that they would be spared further outbreaks of bubonic plague (1 Samuel 6:1–9). This suggests that they had spotted that the cause of plague was in some way connected with flea-infested rodents.

When it came to internal disorders and other infections they were completely at a loss, and tended to hand these over to magicians and soothsayers, although the religious leaders did much to discourage this pagan practice.

Their forté lay in what we nowadays might call the surgery of trauma, as they were skilled in dealing with injuries and war wounds. For example, historians report the incident when King Joram 'returned to the city of Jezreel to recover from his wounds' which the Syrians had given him at Ramoth (2 Kings 8:29). Again the prophet Isaiah resorts to surgical language to describe the plight of the Israelites when he says 'You are covered with bruises and sores and open wounds. Your wounds have not been cleaned or bandaged. No ointment has been put on them' (Isaiah 1:6).

In spite of many wars and battles, the Israelites were a caring people who looked after their war wounded and their elderly citizens. Because of their abhorrence of practical anatomy, it would be easy to assume that their surgical practice was little more than first aid, or at the most patching up. On the contrary, the Hebrews embarked on heroic operations such as trepanning, that is, boring holes in the skull, presumably to release demons in those suspected of demon possession, or to reduce intra-cranial pressure following injury to the head. One can only gasp at such horrendous treatment undertaken without anaesthetic or antiseptics and with only the crudest of instruments. Yet, on the evidence of at least one skull dating from around the eighth century BC, the patient survived. Not only that, but there is also evidence of bone regeneration (Heaton 1956).

Psalms 6, 22, 88 and 102 give a vivid impression of ill-health and physical hardship. The climate, the dust and the flies gave rise to skin irritations and eye troubles, and of course plague was endemic. As if that was not enough there was famine, drought and often starvation. The extremes of climate exacerbated poor and inadequate water supplies, which in turn gave rise to all manner of digestive problems, plus dysentery and malaria.

Black's Bible Dictionary (1959) lists over twenty medical conditions mentioned in the Old Testament. Further evidence from Egyptian papyrus records shows that they were also familiar with tuberculosis and poliomyelitis, facts further verified from recent post-mortem examinations carried out on Egyptian mummies (Heaton 1956).

Although much here appears to be gloom and doom, yet there were highlights to remind us of the healing hand of God, though not all of this is recorded in the Old Testament, nor is it directly associated with the Hebrews.

The so-called pagan nations were also having their successes in the field of medicine and surgery, as we shall see.

To conclude with we are reminded of Hezekiah, healed of his boil by the prophet Isaiah and restored to full health. He had received a deputation from the sovereign of the Babylonians, on his return to health. To show the measure of his fitness Hezekiah entertained his visitors in a manner befitting a royal prince and his retinue. 'About this time, the king of Babylonia, Merodach Baladan, son of Baladan, heard that King Hezekiah had been ill, so he sent him a letter and a present. Hezekiah welcomed the messengers and showed them his wealth – his silver and gold, his spices and perfumes, and all his military equipment. There was nothing in his storerooms or anywhere in his kingdom that he did not show them' (Isaiah 39:1–2). Such a tour is evidence enough of a good recovery.

3

The healing miracles of Jesus and of the early church

As we leave the healing miracles of the Old Testament, we see the continuance of God's healing grace in the person of Jesus, his Son. Here we have God entering right into the midst of human suffering.

Although there is more to Christ's earthly ministry than the healing of our bodies, Jesus uses his healing ministry not only to relieve suffering but also as a means of showing us something of his Father's compassion and concern for us as individuals. He focuses on our diseases and afflictions in order to bring us into a personal relationship with himself and with his Father. The healing miracles were not ends in themselves, but were a part of his overall plan aimed at the ultimate salvation of a fallen race.

With the healing miracles, I have endeavoured to update the medical nomenclature, wherever possible, to demonstrate that many of the diseases and afflictions suffered by people in and around the time of Jesus were little different from those suffered by people nowadays, even if the names were slightly different. I have also added some notes to clarify certain obscure conditions.

The illnesses on which Jesus performed his healing miracles can be classified into three distinct groups. They are:

a Those which are made up of physical or organic disorders.
b Those which are nervous or neurological in origin.

c Those which are nervous or neurological but which also reveal deep psychological problems.

In the first group I have listed the following:

1. One leper healed (Mark 1:40–45); (Matthew 8:1–4); (Luke 5:12–14).
2. Ten lepers healed (Luke 17:11–19). Leprosy was a general term used in and around Palestine to denote any serious skin affliction during the time of our Lord. The references here might just as easily have been psoriasis (Hastings 1933).
3. The woman with the haemorrhage (Mark 5:25–34); (Matthew 9:20–22); (Luke 8:43–48). Depending on her age, this woman could well have been suffering from menorrhagia or post-menopausal bleeding.
4. The blind man at Bethsaida (Mark 8:22–26).
5. Blind Bartimaeus (Mark 10:46–52); (Luke 18:35–43); (Matthew 20:29–34). This is probably the same incident that is mentioned above (in 4), although Matthew mentions two men (Weatherhead 1968).
6. The man born blind (John 9:1–41); (Matthew 9:27). Matthew refers to two men, but both references could well be to the same incident (Weatherhead 1968).

Blindness was exceedingly common in and around Palestine (Grant and Rowley 1973). There were two main forms: trachoma, a highly contagious form of conjunctivitis transmitted by lice; and optic atrophy as found in old people such as Isaac (Genesis 27).

7. The man with dropsy (Luke 14:2). This man could have been suffering from chronic heart disease or any condition which would cause oedema, and not as a punishment from God for continued wilful sin, especially self-indulgence (Hastings 1933). This latter was the current thinking at that time.
8. Peter's mother-in-law (Mark 1:29–31); (Matthew 8:14–15); (Luke 4:38–39). The fever could have been caused by malaria or pneumonia.
9. The deaf mute (Mark 7:32–37).
10. The centurion's servant and/or the nobleman's son (Matthew 8:5–13); (Luke 7:1–10); (John 4:46–54). These two accounts are perhaps of the same incident. There is nothing

here to suggest what they were suffering from, but the symptoms suggest that it might have been tetanus. Both were in great pain and at the point of death (Grant and Rowley 1973).

In the second group I would list the following:

11. The man by Bethesda's (or Bethzatha) pool (John 5:1–18). We are not told what form the illness took. One suggestion is a degenerative disease affecting the spinal cord, such as locomotor ataxia (Grant and Rowley 1973), but the fact that it was of long duration tends to exclude this.

12. The woman whom Satan had bound over (Luke 13:10–17). Her spirit of infirmity could have been severe spinal curvature with fusion of the vertebrae – spondylitis deformans. This could have been tuberculous or arthritic in origin.

13. The man with the withered hand (Mark 3:1–6); (Matthew 12:9–14); (Luke 6:6–11). This was perhaps some form of atrophy affecting bones and muscles.

14. The paralytic at Capernaum (Mark 2:1–12); (Matthew 9:1–8); (Luke 5:18–26). This may have been a disease of the central nervous system, such as lesion of the spinal cord or the result of poliomyelitis.

In the third group we see:

15. The Gerasene demoniac (Mark 5:1–20); (Matthew 8:28–34); (Luke 8:26–39).

16. The man 'possessed' at Capernaum (Mark 1:23–28); (Luke 4:33–37).

17. The dumb and blind demoniac (Matthew 9:32–33; 12:22); (Luke 11:14).

The first three in this group have severe mental illness. The use of the words 'demoniac' and 'possessed' suggests an inability to cope with reality, and is probably indicative of some form of psychosis. The third in this group has the additional problem of dumbness and blindness.

18. The daughter of the Syro–Phoenician woman (Mark 7:24–30); (Matthew 15:21–28).

19. The epileptic boy (Mark 9:14–29); (Matthew 17:14–21); (Luke 9:37–43).

14   SUFFERING AND THE CONTEMPLATIVE

The last two appear to be suffering from severe epilepsy.

All of Christ's healing miracles are included above with the exception of Lazarus, the brother of Martha and Mary (John 11:3, 11, 36, 38–44), and of Jairus's daughter (Mark 5:35–42); (Luke 8:53–55). In both of these incidents Jesus is more deliberate in his actions. He not only heals, he restores to life.

Finally we have the healing of the ear of Malchus, servant of the High Priest (Luke 22:49–51); (John 18:10). During the scuffle in the garden when one of the disciples struck the slave and cut off his ear, Jesus touched the man's ear and healed him. This is an instance of what surgeons might call healing by first intention; put more accurately, it is healing by divine intention.

There are those who like to consider the healing miracles of Jesus in the light of their so-called psychological involvement. Although I am prepared to believe that some of the afflictions that Jesus healed were psychologically based, particularly those mentioned in group three, I am not prepared to accept that all the Jesus-healing miracles had some sort of neurotic tendency about them. To look at them in this light gives the psychic part, where it is present, far greater importance than it deserves. Admittedly the five in the third category had deep psychological and emotional problems, but if we lump all the healing miracles together in the light of some vague psychic phenomenon, then we are in danger of believing that all the afflictions which Jesus healed were psychosomatic in origin. This most Christians would find very hard to accept. It would further tend to make Jesus look like a psychotherapist, instead of the Son of God.

Jesus was unique in that he was not during his earthly life an extension of all that was best in the conventional Jewish healing tradition; neither was he some sort of diagnostician-cum-therapist who was very much in advance of His time. No, Jesus was incomparable, because he was the embodiment of the divine presence who was able to see beyond diagnostic skills and therapeutic remedies, right into the heart of suffering humanity with love and tenderness. He was always anxious to relieve suffering and forgive sin wherever he encountered it. This is the Jesus whose healing grace poured from him as if by some sort of conditioned reflex – which in fact it was. Yet, the healing miracles of Jesus, as we have already said, were never ends in themselves but rather part of a greater purpose. We glimpse this through his deliberate aversion to any form of ostentation, and the stern way in which he discouraged sensationalism. Love and compassion compelled him to heal the sick, but his ultimate aim was the salvation of souls.

Healing miracles of the early church

With the Fall at the first apostasy, humankind forfeited not only its innocence but also its immunity against disease and infection. The human race had become susceptible to all known afflictions and had stepped into a veritable minefield from which there was no apparent relief or escape. I say, apparent relief or escape, because but for the grace of God, the human race as we know it could well have become extinct. The potential was certainly there. Instead an all-forgiving Father set about the task of showing his people the best way to deal with disease and how to avoid it:

If you will obey me completely by doing what I consider right and by keeping my commands, I will not punish you with any of the diseases that I brought on the Egyptians. I am the Lord, the one who heals you.

(Exodus 15:26).

Much of God's instruction to his people on how to remain healthy is contained in the Mosaic Law, although the ancient Semitic rite of circumcision dates back to the covenant which God had made with Abraham (Genesis 17:10–12). Several theories have been advanced to explain this ancient custom but hygienic considerations must always be among them.

Many of the health rules were based upon simple, common-sense rules of physical cleanliness such as the washing of the hands and feet before and after eating (John 13:6ff); and especially after returning from the market (Mark 7:4). Personal hygiene was also encouraged through frequent bathing (2 Samuel 11:2); and ritual bathing as at the Pool of Bethesda was used both for cleansing as well as for healing purposes (John 5:1–18).

Other rules concerned sexual behaviour (Leviticus 12, 15, 19); the disposal of excreta (Deuteronomy 23:10–14); and the prevention and care of leprosy and other skin diseases and also bodily discharges (Leviticus 13, 14, 15).

There were strict laws about food and about animals that were fit for human consumption (Leviticus 11:1–46). The general rule was that such animals must have hooves; this therefore excluded rodents, reptiles and carnivores. Furthermore, the hooves must be cloven, and cloven-footed creatures must chew the cud. This excluded the camel and the rabbit, although the latter should really be included with rodents.

Fish, for example, must have fins and scales; shellfish were thus excluded. Birds must not be of the carnivorous varieties. This same God showed his concern in many other ways, not least of all in his healing miracles of the Old Testament, in the healing miracles of Jesus, and finally in those of the early church.

The healing miracles of the early church were in fact an extension of Christ's own healing ministry. Just as the healing miracles of Jesus were never ends in themselves, so we find that Jesus sent forth his disciples not only to heal the sick but also to preach salvation to souls. 'He called the twelve disciples together and sent them out two by two. He gave them authority over evil spirits. . . So they went out and preached that people should turn away from their sins. They drove out many demons, and rubbed olive-oil on many sick people and healed them' (Mark 6:7, 12–13). Again St Luke the physician states: 'Jesus called the twelve disciples together and gave them power and authority to drive out all demons and to cure diseases. Then he sent them out to preach the Kingdom of God and to heal the sick. . . The disciples left and travelled through all the villages, preaching the Good News and healing people everywhere' (Luke 9:1–2, 6).

'After this the Lord chose another seventy-two men and sent them out two by two, to go ahead of him to every town and place where he himself was about to go. He said to them, "There is a large harvest, but few workers to gather it in . . . heal the sick in that town, and say to the people there, 'The Kingdom of God has come near to you'." The seventy-two men came back in great joy. "Lord," they said, "even the demons obeyed us when we gave them a command in your name!" ' (Luke 10:1–2, 9, 17).

Again, all of this would appear to support our earlier assumption that, important as the healing miracles were, they must always be subordinate in importance to the need for salvation, or to put it more precisely, the healing of souls. None the less all of this is further evidence of the healing hand of God at work, even if the emphasis appears to be more on the healing of souls.

After the Ascension, we find in the Acts of the Apostles how the few were able to cure many diseases in the name of the Lord. 'Many miracles and wonders were being done through the apostles, and everyone was filled with awe' (Acts 2:43). 'Many miracles and wonders were being performed among the people by the apostles' (Acts 5:12). 'Stephen, full of grace and power, wrought great wonders and signs' (Acts 6:8).

With Philip in Samaria, 'Evil spirits came out from many people with a loud cry, and many paralysed and lame people were healed. So there was great joy in that city' (Acts 8:7–8). Again in the same chapter, 'Simon himself also believed; and after being baptised, he stayed close to Philip and was astounded when he saw the great wonders and miracles that were being performed' (Acts 8:13). We turn to Barnabas and Paul, who report 'all the miracles and wonders that God had performed through them among the Gentiles' (Acts 15:12). Acts 28:9 touches on the healing ministry of Paul on the island of Malta. 'When this happened, all the other sick people on the island came and were healed'.

The famous text from the letter from St James (5:14–15) reads 'Is there anyone who is ill? He should send for the church elders, who will pray for him and rub olive-oil on him in the name of the Lord. This prayer made in faith will heal the sick person'.

Also in Malta, 'Publius's father was in bed, sick with fever and dysentery. Paul went into his room, prayed, placed his hands on him, and healed him. When this happened, all the other sick people on the island came and were healed' (Acts 28:8–9).

The healing of the lame man at the Gate Beautiful (Acts 3:2–10); here the patient is described as a pauper, who uses his lameness to make a living. He may well have been suffering from congenital club foot or spina bifida (Grant and Rowley 1963). When Peter and John said, 'Look at us!' he paid attention, expecting to get something in the way of alms. The forcefulness of Peter's manner cured not only his lameness but also his desire to go begging.

We notice an interesting departure later, when patients are cured by the shadow of Peter, and by handkerchiefs which had touched Paul (Acts 5:15–16; 19:12). This could well have been the first record of healing by means of a sacred relic. Again, in the catacombs of Rome, where many Christian martyrs and saints were buried, Christian pilgrims used to come to venerate their remains. Many took away oil from the lamps burning in the shrines, believing this to have some beneficial effect. They also touched the tombs and remains of the saints with handkerchiefs, and these they carried away as relics, and subsequently used them to bring about healing miracles. This practice endured until many centuries later, when the bodies were removed and re-interred in the basilicas of the city.

Ananias restored the sight of Paul (Acts 9:17). Paul's blindness, which followed his conversion, may well have been a hysterical reaction by his body to all the emotional upheaval he was going through at the time of his conversion, as well as to the events leading up to this episode. Subsequently the words of Ananias, delivered with the Lord's authority, were sufficient to redress the balance and restore his eyesight. Be that as it may, it was all part of the plan that God had prepared for his servant Paul, in order to bring healing and truth to his people.

On the occasion when Peter healed Aeneas of palsy (Acts 9:32–34), Aeneas was doubtless aware of the many healing miracles that were occurring around him. Weatherhead (1968) suggests that healing might well have been due to conversion hysteria, (the term hysteria being used in its technical sense and not in any loose, disparaging way).

Paul's healing of a cripple at Lystra (Acts 14:8–10) is another example of the authoritative way in which the Apostle was able to bring healing grace to bear on the sufferer. In a loud voice, he said 'Stand up straight on your feet', but although the patient responded, he did not try to walk. Strong suggestion from Paul persuaded the patient to walk (Weatherhead 1968).

The exorcism of a maid with a spirit of divination (Acts 16:16–18) was a fortuitous matter for the girl. Paul brought the healing grace of Jesus to bear upon her, probably because he felt irritated by her repeated interruptions. The girl kept saying 'These men are servants of the Most High God'. Her healing was to cost Paul and Silas dearly as they were imprisoned for their pains.

After the healing miracles of Jesus, and those of the early church, evidence suggests that the further we move from Pentecost, the more tenuous becomes the church's healing ministry. Those miracles that were performed demanded more from the one being healed by way of prayers and fasting, and less from the healer. Sadly, the spontaneity of Christ's healing grace had all but vanished. It was as though a less powerful force was at work.

Furthermore, many of the miracles recorded by the doctors and the saints of the church during the first three centuries seemed often to be related to the use of holy relics and anointing with oil taken from the lamps in shrines and sanctuaries. Again this tends to imply that much of the healing depended rather upon the faith of the individual and less upon the church or the healer.

Although the healing ministry of the church was much diminished, it was never completely lost. Such, of course, can be said of the church's healing ministry in all ages, because there have always been individuals who, through the grace of God and the love of Jesus, together with deep personal faith, have been able to bring back health to the sick.

4

Other early influences and their contribution to medical care

During the time of the Old Testament Hebrews, right up to the healing ministry of Jesus and that of the early church, several dynasties were to make their mark on medical practice. These were the Egyptians, the Mesopotamians, the Babylonians and the Greeks as well as others. To begin with, all had certain similarities in the realms of mysticism, which were akin to the practice of medicine. All believed that demons and evil spirits were the chief cause of disease and infection. As already seen, this was one probable reason for the operation of trepanning of the skull and supposed release of evil spirits ostensibly under the control of the gods. The presence of disease meant that the gods had withdrawn their favour, and the demons and evil spirits were presumably free to do their worst. The converse of this was also true, in that good health meant that you were being looked on with favour by the gods and there was no need to placate them, at least for the present.

Mesopotamia

It was in Mesopotamia that the first tentative steps were taken to put medicine on a scientific basis. Until then medicine, magic and religion were very closely linked. The mystical element was first cast aside in Mesopotamia when the causes of accidents and injuries were recognised and a more rational attitude to disease and infection adopted. Progress in medical science at that time did not confine itself to matters strictly medical, but borrowed frequently from other disciplines. Embalming and mummifying played a significant part, and gave practical instruction in anatomy. It was through the embalmers that medical men learned from the Egyptians that the heart and the blood vessels played a very important part in supporting life.

Babylonia

The Babylonians, on the other hand, knew the value of discussion in ascertaining a correct diagnosis. The sick were taken into the market place where they discussed with others their symptoms and the probable cause of their illness. This in turn often led to a correct diagnosis and subsequent prognosis. Once the link between medicine and religion had been loosened, and the belief accepted that disease and disorders had specific causes, so the quest for medical solutions increased.

The Babylonians had advanced in practical terms and knew about the art of splinting fractured bones. This they did by use of glue-soaked bandages. They also knew how to close deep wounds by using strips of linen anchored to healthy skin, which drew the edges of a wound into apposition.

They further recognised the connection between guilt and fear and their deleterious effect upon health in general.

The availability of treatment in Babylon varied and generally speaking was confined to cities and large towns. It was invariably a costly business and was only available to the rich. Soldiers were treated free, and sometimes slaves had the benefit of being treated by their master's physician with the serious drawback that they could be regarded as guinea pigs, and used for experimentation to try out new treatments (Coleman 1985).

Attempts to introduce a code of ethics into the practice of medicine were made not by a doctor or a priest but by King Hammurabi, who ruled Babylonia *circa* 2000 BC and who prepared a series of rules designed to protect doctors and patients (Coleman 1985). These included a list of fees to be charged for items of service and penalties for professional misconduct and incompetence. The penalties could be heavy and included the loss of fingers and even the loss of life depending on the severity of the infringement. Penalties relating to malpractice against slaves were correspondingly lighter.

The Babylonians also showed some evidence of specialisation in anatomy, surgery, gynaecology and ophthalmology, and various texts were prepared and used in these subjects. Treatment of obscure conditions recommended that the physician treat the condition for three days with a particular remedy, before resorting to another form of treatment.

There was also the beginnings of a public health system and rules were meant to be observed on the proximity of houses and dwelling places to that of cattle. There were rules about the disposal of the dead, and the disposal of clothing belonging to those suffering from infectious diseases. In addition there were rules designed to protect the purity of public water supplies (Coleman 1985).

China

Looking further east towards China, we find religious belief prevented the drawing of blood and the mutilation of the body, so that virtually no progress was made in surgery. Oriental medicine, and in particular the medical practice of the Chinese, was more passive by nature and consisted largely of herbal remedies. They were familiar with massage and other manipulative treatments. These became well established and were often the main form of treatment for physical ailments together with acupuncture. The Chinese attached great importance to diagnostic skills, and recognised the significance of changes in the radial pulse in the management and treatment of fevers, of which they were familiar with many. They also established the art of finger printing and knew of its importance in identifying the individual.

India

Still in the east and still contemporary with the Jewish patriarchs and the tribes of Israel, the Hindus in India carried out a remarkably high standard of medical practice. Their knowledge and expertise in the field of surgery are almost akin to that of early twentieth-century surgical practice in Europe. Their surgical techniques were well in advance of anything being carried out by Jew, Mesopotamian or Babylonian. They had no less than one hundred different types of surgical instruments ranging over scalpels, needles, scissors, hooks and catheters. They were familiar with infection control – a factor probably responsible for their high success rate in surgical procedures, and also reflected in the high standards of cleanliness in their operating theatres. Surgeons and their staffs were encouraged to keep their finger nails short and their hands well scrubbed. Sheets were steam cleaned and instruments boiled. Operating staff wore clean white overgarments. Surgeons also used anaesthetics and antiseptics (Coleman 1985). It was a most remarkable, if not incomprehensible state of affairs, since it was to be several thousand years before these advantages were to reach the medical scene in the Western world.

The Hindus also had sophisticated and enlightened ideas about convalescence and knew the advantages of good food, fresh air and proper rest. To counteract waterborne infection, they practised boiling and filtering by use of coarse sand, gravel and charcoal, a system which shows strong similarities to present-day filter beds used in the purification of public water supplies.

Evidence also suggests that they practised a form of preventive medicine and inoculated against smallpox; used mosquito nets to control malaria; and recognised that there was a connection between plague and rats.

We now move closer to the early Christian era to look at two contemporary civilisations – that of the Greeks and that of the Romans.

During the period leading up to the Christian era and during the early centuries of Christian civilisation, we have a somewhat antithetical situation between materialistic medical practice on the one hand, and the decline of the Church's healing ministry on the other hand. One cannot be too specific here about dates and events because there is much overlapping between the main contestants. For example the great age of the Greeks began some five hundred years BC with the revolt of the Ionian Greek cities against the Persian King Darius (*circa* 499 BC) and was to continue until

Greek civilisation succumbed to Roman influence some two hundred years later. The Roman Empire itself was also to see its own demise with the sack of Rome by Alaric the Goth in AD 410. During this whole period, almost a thousand years, we see the rise and fall of two empires, and right in the middle the healing ministry of Jesus and that of the early church.

During the first centuries of the church's history, we see the first real evidence of a decline in its healing ministry. St Cyprian (200–58 AD) wrote, 'The sins of Christians have weakened the power of the Church', although the early church rationalised and made excuses that God had withdrawn the gift given to the apostles, or that he no longer willed to heal and that Christians had 'to bear their sufferings as Christ His cross' (Weatherhead 1968).

St Augustine (AD 354–430) has it on record that some miracles were happening occasionally, but that this was the exception rather than the rule. Similarly, St Chrysostom (AD 357–407) speaks of the sporadic nature of the healing miracles. However, although evidence suggests a definite decline in the church's healing ministry, there is also much evidence to suggest that it was never completely absent. St Ambrose (AD 340–97), Bishop of Milan, records an incident where a blind man was healed by touching a holy relic that had been in contact with two martyrs. The theologian Tertullian (AD 155–230) speaks of healing miracles being carried out and even gives instances of the dead being raised to life.

With the other contestants, the Greeks and the Romans, we see the influence of medical matters gradually gaining in importance, first during the pre-Christian era, then right through Christ's ministry and that of the early church, and continuing for many centuries even after the fall of the Roman Empire. Much of this influence was due entirely to Greek thinking and philosohy; and although the Romans were neither scientists nor philosophers their contribution to the medical scene was none the less significant.

The Greeks

The Greeks, by their geographical position, were, in effect, a trading nation with contacts which took them well beyond the Mediterranean. By nature, they were philosophical in their thinking with the added ability of being able to absorb ideas and theories belonging to others, and turning them to practical use.

There seems to be little doubt that when dealing with ideas and discoveries which belonged to others in the first instance, they were able to transform what was often hypothetical and abstract into something real, scientific and meaningful. With borrowed ideas, for example from the Hindus, they had deduced the importance of cleanliness, sleep and a healthy diet for the care and nurture of the sick. They also laid great emphasis on the mobilising of the body's own natural defences in convalescence, plus their own added health rules. They found or borrowed massage and incorporated this into mud bath therapies, and began what can only be called the Greek equivalent of modern-day health farms.

In 460 BC, the first of the Greek philosophical giants was born on the island of Cos. His name was Hippocrates, and he was to become known universally as the Father of Medicine. His main contribution was to separate medicine from religion and abstract philosophy (Coleman 1985).

This was a courageous act, and although much of his philosophy has of course been superseded, none the less it could be said that he did for medicine at that time what St Paul did for New Testament theology. He believed that the physician should look for natural rather than supernatural causes for diseases and other afflictions. He was a meticulous worker and wrote copious notes and case histories for the various diseases he encountered. He also paid strict attention to all the signs and manifestations of disease processes, and gave a very accurate account of puerperal septicaemia, malaria and dysentery. He was probably the first to recognise that epilepsy was a disease of the central nervous system, and that insanity was a disease rather than a supernatural affliction sent by the gods.

Hippocrates knew the value of clean water, which he had boiled, and suggested its use for cleansing wounds. He also knew that linen strips soaked in wine had certain antiseptic properties when applied to wounds.

His knowledge of anatomy was superficial, as he considered the human body to be sacrosanct, and was therefore not in favour of dissection as an aid to practical anatomy. This attitude he incorporated into his Hippocratic Oath, where physicians, among other things, promised not to use the knife on their patients.

We turn now to another genius of Greek civilisation – Aristotle (384–322 BC). He was a scientist, philosopher and one time pupil of Plato. Aristotle took the whole field of knowledge as his subject, gave it integrity and created a philosophy that was to last for close on two thousand years. His main contribution to medical science was the founding of comparative anatomy and embryology. His sketches and notes on human anatomy were derived from dissections carried out on executed criminals. He also collaborated with other philosophers and was to some extent responsible for producing the then new discipline of physiology. When he died the world of medicine was much the poorer, because there was no one able to equal him in intellectual stature, and although there were other philosophers at that time who made worthy contributions, none equalled Aristotle in importance.

The Romans

With the decline of the Greek Empire, the Roman Empire went through a phase of expansion, and by the year 31 BC Octavian (later known as Augustus) had become the unchallenged master of the Roman world. Roman influence was then growing in size and importance.

The two cultures were quite different. The Greeks attached much importance to philosophy, art and science, whereas the Romans were essentially practical and excelled at engineering and road making and in military matters. Their practice of medical matters was fairly basic and revolved around the head of the household who kept a medicine chest. Medicaments and remedies, such as they were, were only dispensed as a last resort. The Greeks were to change this. With the overthrow of the Greek Empire, many Greek physicians were captured and shipped off as slaves to Rome. Although kept as slaves, many continued to practise their medical skills. Unfortunately, although trained in Greece, some abandoned the Hippocratic theories and teachings of Aristotle and quickly became absorbed into the mysticism of the Roman gods. Fortunately, this was only a temporary phase and soon many returned to the theories and practices they had learned from their master. Slowly, Greek physicians began to earn respect from their Roman owners and by 46 BC Julius Caesar granted Roman citizenship to all doctors of medicine. Later Caesar Augustus introduced a decree exempting all surgeons and physicians from paying taxes. The new-found prosperity enjoyed by the medical men unfortunately attracted the unscrupulous, with the result that there was a falling off in standards. This then forced the authorities to introduce in AD 200 a licensing system for all doctors engaged in medical practice.

About this time there arose a Roman physician by the name of Claudius Galen (AD 131–201). Galen was of Greek parents and was trained in Greece but like many of his contemporaries was to find himself in Rome where his skill as a surgeon was recognised, and he was appointed surgeon to the School of Gladiators. Galen was greatly influenced by the theories of Aristotle and in particular his theories on the heart and circulation. His knowledge of anatomy he learned mainly from his work as a military surgeon. His understanding of physiology and pathology was advanced for his time and was based on the hypothesis of the 'four humours'.

The 'humours', broadly speaking, were blood, phlegm, yellow bile and black bile. Galen believed that illness was caused through the imbalance of the humours, and that treatment centred around the correction of the imbalance. His speculation about the humours may have been borrowed from the Chinese, Hindus or the Egyptians, but in any case Galen attempted to give it dignity. He also systematised medical knowledge in general, and he may well have been the first medical man to recognise that medical science has a rightful part to play in religious affairs, a concept he linked with his own ideas of purposive creation through the will of God. His theories were to last for over a thousand years.

Although the Romans did not give much time or thought to clinical medicine, their engineering and military skills did much to advance the cause of public health through the building of aqueducts, sewers and baths. While Galen was engaged in his duties as a military surgeon, Rome was served by fourteen great aqueducts which supplied the citizens with no less than 300 million gallons of drinking water each day. Plumbing was much valued, and most houses were furnished with a private cistern, running water and a flushing closet (Coleman 1985).

As Rome was the centre of government, soldiers, politicians, diplomats and other dignitaries made it their home base while travelling abroad. As these officials returned from foreign tours of duty, they brought with them many diseases and infections new to the permanent residents. Since the latter had no natural immunity or resistance to these various infections, the initial outbreaks soon became epidemics. Smallpox and measles, unrecognised as such, became rampant. Malaria was also evident. It is ironic that hundreds of years before the Hindus had recognised the connection between malaria and the mosquito and had taken the necessary steps to control it. This piece of knowledge seems to have passed the Romans by, and as with other infections they found that military might was unable to deal with these new adversaries. The fabric of Roman society was severely dented. The populace felt disillusioned with the so-called invincibility of the glorious empire, with the professed herbal remedies and with the Roman gods, all of which were no match for the recurrent epidemics and subsequent deterioration in living standards. In desperation they looked for new reliable medical ideas, for a new religion to replace the gods, in fact, for a new system of belief. They turned to Christianity (Weatherhead 1968).

As we have seen, for some considerable time before the advent of Christianity, medical care in the Middle East and the Orient broadly speaking fell into two main categories. There was the medical care administered by the religious authorities which was essentially confined to the Israelites and later to the Christian communities; and secular medical care essentially confined to the gentile nations. Both existed side by side in their separateness, and it is perhaps not difficult to see how this dichotomy evolved and persisted. In early history, medical care was a strange mixture of religion, magic and mysticism. The Jewish Patriarchs did much to rid religion of the superstitious element. In singling out and purifying the religious element they consequently separated themselves from mainstream medical practice. Jewish or religious medical care became very much the concern of the religious authorities and therefore developed along the lines of religious bias. The secular medical authorities for different reasons also managed to cast aside magic and mysticism, simply because they recognised the connection between disease and infection, accidents and injury, and it is here that the dichotomy begins. As a result the two forms of medical care were either religiously or scientifically orientated. Both developed along their own particular pathways.

It is tempting to think that since the Jews and Christians supposedly had the prerogative in religious affairs, secular medical care, essentially gentile, must therefore have had no apparent religious connection. Yet it would be wrong to assume such a lack. The religion of the Hindus, for example, 'is a tireless quest for truth . . . and that truth is God' (New Catechism 1970). Does this then make the Hindu in terms of religious devotion any different from the Jew who worships Yahweh, the God of truth; or from the Christian who acknowledges Jesus to be 'the way, the truth, and the life' (John 14:6)? Perhaps this reason alone explains why the Hindus were so adept and advanced in terms of surgical expertise. Theirs was an enlightened form of scientific care. Similarly, the Jews and the Christians, worshipping the same God of truth, had their successes also with the healing miracles, which reached the pinnacle of success, by a religious route, in the person of Jesus.

We further glimpse this quest for truth with the Greek philosophers and again later with the collapse of the Roman Empire, whose citizens had become disillusioned with paganism. Although religion and science were to continue their separate identities, both had this insatiable desire for truth, and sought to incorporate the truth into their medical practice.

It was several generations before humankind would combine the two attributes of religious faith and scientific knowledge which would then enable them to bridge the gap and end the dichotomy. Even then the transition would be incomplete for many, although there have always been those who have found no difficulty in combining the two.

5

Medical practice in medieval times

With the collapse of the Roman Empire political and social life in Europe was thrown into chaos. Nowhere was this more evident than in the realms of medical practice. Many of the advances made by the Romans in public health, sanitation, and sewerage were abandoned; the surgical skills learned from the Indians and the aptness learned from the Greek physicians were also lost; and although many of the texts were to be stored in the monastic archives, they were to remain there for close on a thousand years.

With chaos, plagues and infections became endemic. Famine was often rife, and in addition the medieval church had lost much of its original impetus. Disease and illness were once again considered to be caused by God as a direct result of sin. Subsequently, the study of anatomy, physiology and pathology were openly discouraged by the ecclesiastical authorities on the grounds that, since disease was thought to be sent from God, its relief could only be obtained through prayer and worship. Further, since the church at that time also believed in the physical resurrection of the body at the day of judgement, dissection and the study of human anatomy were wholeheartedly disapproved of.

For close on a millenium no progress was made in medical science, and much of this was due entirely to misguided and often unenlightened religious belief.

In history books, this period is known as the Middle Ages or medieval period and extended from around AD 400 to 1500. In the world of medical science it was an age of scholasticism, an age when it was thought that everything in the realms of science that had to be learned, had already been learned.

The function of scholars became that of reading, preserving and transcribing manuscripts into the international language of the day, which was Latin. This explains, to some extent, the continuing influence of Galen in those medical matters which had managed to survive (Rhodes 1985). It also explains the continuing authority of the church not only in religious and political matters, but now also in medical matters. With hindsight, it is perhaps easy to see how this arose. The clergy had the monopoly of knowledge and education. They also had access to the libraries and of course could read and write, unlike many of their contemporaries. This all-pervasive authority of the church was not conducive to scientific thought, let alone medical practice.

One could be excused for thinking the church's influence on medieval medicine was entirely destructive, but this would not be true. In spite of the aridity and the scholasticism, this enforced hiatus did much to re-enforce the Christian belief, in medical matters, that the individual was important in the sight of God irrespective of colour, class or creed. This philosophy, shared by church and medicine alike, had a practical outlet in caring for patients, and is perhaps the first indication that the dichotomy between the two great disciplines was after all capable of being bridged, even if this was only a tentative step in the right direction.

The care of patients began during the many and often varied epidemics of the time and seemed to rest mainly, in the first instance, with the religious authorities. The clergy and many charitably disposed lay people did much to ease the suffering of the sick and dying by making available the infirmaries attached to monasteries, abbeys and convents as well as private houses belonging to the well-to-do. These religious houses provided a safe haven with creature comforts, nursing care and devotion as well as herbal remedies and prayer; in fact, places that were at last being set aside for the specific purpose of caring for the sick and dying. One notable example was the Hôtel-Dieu in Paris which was founded by Bishop Landry in the seventh century (Coleman 1985) and staffed by Parisian ladies. Later these women were organised into a sisterhood by Pope Innocent IV, and may well have been the first nursing order of nuns. Other examples led to the laying down of two religious foundations in London – that of St Bartholomew's Hospital in 1123 and of St Thomas's Hospital in 1215.

Many saints were associated with the healing ministry – St Jerome, St Augustine, St Cuthbert and others. Most of them were familiar with the use of holy water and chrism (consecrated oil). Their cures were many and ranged from snake bites to all manner of internal disorders. It is believed that some bishops were also trained physicians, and the Seventh Canon of Hippolytus (fourth century) contains a prayer for the ordination of bishops, which says:

'Grant him, O Lord, to loose all bonds of the iniquity of demons, the power to heal all diseases and quickly to beat down Satan under his feet'.

(C.G. Dawson 1935)

Towards the end of the age of scholasticism, when the church's healing ministry was still in evidence, we have the example of two Arab Christians who were perhaps unique – SS Cosmas and Damian. These medieval saints, both brothers and martyrs, are credited with many cures especially in the practice of surgery. Their remarkable piety and surgical expertise succeeded, at least at a personal level, in abolishing the dichotomy between religion and medical science, by combining the technical skill of the surgeon with that of the church's healing ministry. There is a very famous painting which shows the saints transplanting the leg of a black man to a white man. No racial prejudice here!

This is a good place to close the period of medieval medicine, at a point where the saints Cosmas and Damian have succeeded in combining the two disciplines, albeit at a personal level, but none the less in a manner which must confound the sceptics who still think that science and religion cannot be mixed.

6

The Renaissance

The Renaissance marks the change from the Middle Ages to the modern world. This transitional phase, which was spread over many years, began in Italy in the fourteenth century. The word means 'new birth' (Chambers English Dictionary 1988). It signified the dawn of a new era in the world of Italian art, an era which was to extend its influence to the fields of religion, philosophy, poetry, drama, economics, science and technology, including medical science. From Italy the Renaissance spread to France, Germany, Spain and Northern Europe. In Germany we were to see the first stirrings of the religious renaissance, which in turn was to give rise to the Reformation in the sixteenth century. England, for its part, gave birth to the renaissance in poetry. Many ideas and reasons have been offered to explain the phenomenon of re-birth including the fall of Constantinople (1453), the discovery of America (1492) and the discovery of printing, including the first printed version of the bible, known as the Gutenberg Bible, in 1455. Although these doubtless had a bearing, the real cause was simply money, generated by the new merchant classes. They had money to burn and offered some of it by becoming patrons of the arts. In medieval times the patronage of the arts was very much in the hands of the church and art was meant to elevate and instruct, whereas with the Renaissance art was there to delight and give enrichment to life.

The individualism in economic affairs which sprang from the

merchant classes gave rise to a new quest for knowledge and understanding. This questing spirit found its way to the universities and later on into science and technology. The urge for scholarship caused many to question old beliefs and suppositions and gave rise to a separation of clergy and laity at academic level. This separation was in no way adversarial but provided further evidence that the Renaissance was reaching all levels of society.

In medicine the first rumblings of change were found at Salerno on the west coast of Italy, with the establishment of the first medical faculty. Although this pre-dates the Renaissance in art by about two hundred years, there is evidence to suggest that both were connected, as the medical faculty was established with an independence of outlook similar to that which appeared in other medical faculties much later on. Although the Salerno medical school was progressive, it still did not have the advantages of practical anatomy and clung to the old prejudices concerning the sanctity of the human body. It did, however, excel in obstetrics and boasted the first woman obstetrician who did much to advance her subject. Another medical school was opened in Bologna towards the end of the twelfth century, but this time with the advantage that practical anatomy was taught to its students. In 1316 Mundinus wrote a book on the subject (Rhodes 1985).

Further advances in practical anatomy came from an unexpected quarter, that of the artists who produced numerous paintings and sketches of anatomical dissections. The most famous of these were those of Leonardo da Vinci (1452–1519), whose anatomical sketches are renowned for their accuracy.

Soon the advantages of applied anatomy were to be found in the field of surgery and by the sixteenth century surgical procedures were to become gentler and more humane especially in the hands of Ambroise Paré (1510–90). Paré did much to improve the standards of surgery and is credited with a more enlightened attitude towards obstetrics which until then had been in the hands of unqualified midwives. He also combined his surgical and scientific expertise with a deep religious faith, and is remembered for his enlightened saying, 'I dressed him; God healed him' (Rhodes 1985). Here again we have evidence of God's healing hand using the skills and scientific knowledge of yet another faithful servant.

The English Renaissance is characterised in the main by the poetic and literary works of Christopher Marlowe, William Shakespeare and Francis Bacon. These literary giants exemplified all that was new during this golden age of scholarship; but the upsurge in scientific and academic attainments that sprang from the Italian Renaissance was slow to reach England, and when it did, the impact on medical science at first sight appeared in no way extraordinary.

In medicine, this impact took the form of regularising the profession and introduced entrance examinations for the apothecaries, physicians, barber–surgeons and midwives. These changes were fairly rudimentary but were to form the basis for all future developments. Later King Henry VIII authorised the foundation of the two royal colleges – the Royal College of Physicians in 1518 and the Royal College of Surgeons in 1540. With this the physicians and barber–surgeons separated, established their own identity and gained added status through their respective colleges. In time the surgeons separated themselves from the barbers and achieved a further degree of professionalism.

Other changes were the legalising of the apothecaries by Act of Parliament in 1543, and an insistence that all midwives had to be properly qualified. Unfortunately these changes in the first instance were confined to the City of London, and it was several years before these benefits were to become nationwide.

The Renaissance had reached England and the scene was set for the momentous events that lay ahead.

After the Reformation, the next great historical event to follow the Renaissance was undoubtedly the Industrial Revolution. The name was given by the German socialist Friedrich Engels in 1844. He was the son of a wealthy textile manufacturer.

The Industrial Revolution describes the period of change which took place in Britain between broadly 1730 and 1850, but which was to extend its influence to all parts of the Western world and all facets of society – politics, art, religion, literature and morals. In Britain, it transformed a mainly agricultural country, to one predominantly industrial.

This sociological and industrial upheaval began with the mechanisation of the textile industry. Modernisation was brought about with the help of Watt's steam engine, which subsequently laid the foundations for the development of mining and the manufacturing industries. The latter owed their development to the rich mineral resources of coal and iron ore. With the use of the steam engine industry became concentrated around the coalfields, and with the application of scientific principles and business acumen, industry developed and was diversified through the building of canals, bridges, railways and ships. Britain became one of the most prosperous nations in the world.

With this development of industrial output there came a great migration of local populations from the rural areas of England and Wales to the industrial areas of the towns and cities. This population shift produced the most appalling slums. The resultant overcrowding, poor sanitation and inadequate water supplies gave rise to numerous epidemics and a marked decline in standards of health. Deaths among infants, mothers and young adults were unacceptably high. Maternity facilities, where present, were poor and quite unable to cope with the demands being made upon them. Yet, in spite of the high morbidity rate, the population continued to grow. In London alone, the population all but trebled in a period of fifty years.

Working conditions in factories and mills were often squalid and dangerous. The work force was exploited, and augmented by child labour, forced to work long hours and with little pay. On the one hand, the enormous wealth generated by the new industries gave great prosperity to the industrialists, whereas at the other end of the spectrum there was the most abject poverty.

With this increased wealth, nations could afford to maintain large armies and navies to protect their new-found colonial investments. In all during this period wars were being fought on no less than four continents: the Napoleonic Wars which culminated in the Battle of Waterloo (1815); the numerous wars and uprisings in India and Afghanistan (1840s); the Crimean War (1854–56); the American Civil War (1861–65); the Franco–Prussian War (1870–71); and finally the Boer War in South Africa which ended in 1902.

As with all great technical and industrial developments, the Industrial Revolution produced related changes in social life and working conditions. There were the legalising of trade unions and the formation of the Trades Union Congress (1869). There was also much enlightened good will about, which gave rise to various acts in education, public health and housing. Not all of these originated with parliamentarians, but often with public-spirited ordinary people as well as with philanthropists like Lord Shaftesbury (1801–85) and Andrew Carnegie (1835–1918). There were social reformers like Elizabeth Fry (1780–1845) and Thomas Barnardo (1845–1905). Even the novelist Charles Dickens (1812–70) did much to highlight the suffering, deprivation and social injustices of nineteenth-century England.

Against this background of social inequality on the one hand and genuine social reform on the other, we were to see the beginnings of yet another revolution that was to lay the foundations of modern medical practice. It was led in many ways by men of great faith and integrity.

The hand of God, ever present, was again bringing relief to suffering humanity, but this time the divine presence was to find expression in the world of science and discovery.

1 The miracle of transplanting the limb of a black man to a white man by SS Cosmas and Damian, from the painting by Alonso de Sedano

2 Charles Darwin, from an anonymous pen and ink drawing

3   Louis Pasteur, from a portrait by E. Pirou

4   Sir Alexander Fleming, from an anonymous photograph

7

The nineteenth century and the beginnings of the atomic age

The scientific revolution began with a better understanding of molecular structure. The Quaker John Dalton (1766–1844) in his atomic theory stated that matter was made up of indestructible particles called atoms. We were to wait almost a hundred years before scientists would develop the means which would enable them to divide the atomic nucleus or split the atom. Dalton pursued his investigations and postulated that gases expanded when heated. Another scientist, the Italian physicist Amedeo Avogadro (1776–1856), produced his hypothesis which later became known as Avogadro's Law. In this he demonstrated that equal volumes of different gases, under the same conditions of temperature and pressure, contained the same number of molecules. Both of these theories, simple in their context, served to draw chemistry and physics together into the one discipline called physical chemistry, which was to have important repercussions for the years ahead. Nowadays, it would be difficult to explain any biological or scientific principle without recourse to this subject of physical chemistry.

Another step forward in the unification of the basic sciences came with the discoveries of Humphrey Davy (1778–1829), when he isolated the two chemical elements of sodium and potassium by using a phenomenon of physics known as electrolysis. (Davy is better known by the miner's safety lamp with which his name is indelibly linked.)

In 1828 a piece of investigative chemistry enabled Friedrich Wöhler (1800–82) to synthesise the organic compound urea from a purely inorganic source without access to living material. From this it would seem that the biological sciences were inseparable from the world of chemistry and physics. These momentous findings formed the basis of a new discipline called biochemistry, which was to open the gateway to the study of amino acids, proteins and physiology, the latter being the functional basis upon which medical science rests. These discoveries ended much of the speculative empiricism that had characterised medical thinking in the past.

Still in the first half of the nineteenth century, the then professor of experimental physics at Cambridge, Clerk Maxwell (1831–79), while working on the findings of Michael Faraday, published a treatise on his theory of electromagnetic waves. This revolutionised fundamental physics and led Wilhelm Konrad Roentgen (1845–1923) to discover X-rays. Within a few years these were being used as an aid to medical diagnosis.

Further discoveries at this time were those of Antoine Henri Becquerel (1852–1908), who revealed the radioactive properties of uranium. In 1898 the Curies isolated radium from massive quantities of pitchblende. Becquerel and the Curies were to share the Nobel prize in physics for their contribution to that area of medicine known as radiology and oncology, although the medical facility of radiology at that stage was purely diagnostic.

The atom was now beginning to yield its secrets and Johnstone Stoney (1826–1911) gave the name of electrons to the negatively charged particles surrounding the positively charged nucleus of each atom.

Almost in one fell swoop the static world of the ancient philosophers had disappeared for ever, and matter was now seen as a dynamic force. This philosophy forms the basis for all medical and physical sciences. Dynamic concepts of change and evolution were in the minds of many. Maxwell's electromagnetic wave theory gave birth to radiology, radiotherapy, spectroscopy and a host of other specialist subjects and techniques.

The field of practical anatomy gave rise to a deeper understanding of the organs of the human body. The first text book in systematic anatomy was produced over the years 1866–1877 by Jacob Henle (1809–1885) of Zurich.

Physiology was also becoming a specialist subject, and Charles Bell (1774–1842), an eminent surgeon and anatomist, applied his interest to this new specialist field, his main contribution being his work on the physiological function of the spinal cord. Claude Bernard (1813–78), the distinguished French physiologist, did much work on the digestive system, and opened the way for Ivan Pavlov (1849–1936), the Russian physiologist, known for his work on animal behaviour and conditioned reflexes.

So far we have seen a merger between chemistry, physics and the biological sciences. Another fusion was taking place that was to enable humankind to bring unification to the whole chemistry of human experience. It is in this union that we see the hand of God at work with a great sense of purpose, in that the dichotomy between science and religion, so readily accepted in human thinking, was now beginning to crumble. Take the example of the Curies and Wilhelm Roentgen.

The Curies, as Maurice Goldsmith (1971) makes clear, were a frighteningly dedicated family, 'perfectionist beyond belief', as Einstein said of Marie, and often very difficult both to themselves and to other people. Pierre died young in a tragic accident, and both Marie and her daughter Irene died of radiation poisoning, martrys of their own work.

We glimpse something of the spiritual nature of Pierre Curie, although he himself was not formally religious. He enjoyed the company of his brother, and they often holidayed together. As was his custom during these holidays, Pierre would steal away for a spell on his own. Goldsmith says, 'These solitary excursions reinforced his meditative spirit; he forgot all measure of time and pushed himself to extremes. He seemed to rise above all material difficulties'. In some notes he wrote in 1879 he referred to his solitary sojourns: 'Oh, what a fine time I have passed there, in this healing solitude, far from a thousand little worrying things which in Paris have me at their command. No, I do not regret nights spent in the woods, and the days which flow away all alone. If I had time, I would really describe all the dreams I have had. I would describe also my delightful valley, filled with aromatic plants. . . Often I left in the evening and I walked up the valley; I returned with twenty ideas in my head'.

Here we find something of a selfless detachment that the contemplative would do well to imitate; a detachment that recharged his spirit through its meditative silence.

Another facet of this remarkable man's character is his natural humility. He was proposed for an honorary decoration for his contribution to physics by the director of the École, Schutzenberger, who wanted to nominate him for a state decoration, the Palmes académiques. The following is an extract from Pierre Curie's letter, taken from Goldsmith's biography (1971), declining the honour:

'I am informed that you intend to propose me to the Prefect again for decoration. I write to beg you not to do so. If you obtain this decoration for me, you will put me under the obligation of having to refuse it, for I am quite decided never to accept any decoration of any sort. I hope you will be good enough to help me avoid a public declaration which will make me look somewhat ridiculous to many people. If your intention is to give evidence of your interest, you have already done so, and it is a more effective way, by which I have been very moved, in giving me the means to work at ease'.

Such humility and self-effacing commitment, combined with the indomitable spirit of his beloved Marie, enabled them both not only to isolate radium and its healing properties, but also to form the basis of modern-day nuclear physics. Together they identified radioactivity as a property of the disintegrating atom, a discovery which was to prepare the way for a much later venture, nuclear energy.

With Roentgen the conditions were different. Like the Curies, he was a Nobel prize winner, but his entry into physics was almost by accident. He obtained his doctorate at Zurich in 1869, but was uncertain about his future. He already had a diploma in engineering, but, to quote his own words, 'I had two diplomas, one as an engineer and the other as a Ph.D., however, I could not bring myself to go into practical engineering according to the original plan' (Claxton 1970). The young Professor August Kundt, who at that time held a Chair of Physics, solved the problem by inviting Roentgen to try physical science. Thus at the age of twenty-four he began to study and experiment in physics at Zurich. Later he moved to Würzburg University where in 1893 he became rector. In 1895 Roentgen identified X-rays, a discovery which was to mark the beginning of the atomic age. This had a great effect upon the physical sciences. It was also to have a more profound effect upon diagnostic medicine and later radiotherapy.

Roentgen suffered greatly as a result of antisemitism but this cankerous undercurrent did not detract from his idealism both as a scientist and as a man. The following is an extract from his rectorial address given in 1893:

'When the law of nature, hitherto hidden, suddenly emerges from the surrounding fog, when the key, long sought after, to a mechanical combination is found, when the missing link takes its place in a chain of thought, there is then the elation of spiritual victory for the discoverer which by itself alone richly rewards him and lifts him, for a brief moment on to a higher plane. . .'

(Claxton 1970)

These remarks taken with those of Pierre Curie are perhaps a clear indication that neither found any difficulty in correlating their spiritual feelings with those of their scientific principles.

From these brief biographical notes we glimpse something of the personalities of the Curies and that of Wilhem Roentgen. Fuller biographies have been written about all three, but they do not include anything about religious commitment or otherwise. They reveal that none of them was what we would call religious in the formal church-going sense. Marie gave up her Catholicism early in life, and Roentgen was himself a Jew. Yet their personal awareness of a spiritual life beyond that of physical and psychic phenomena is apparent. We see this in Pierre's meditative, solitary sojourns in the countryside; Roentgen's idealism as a scientist in spite of antisemitic attacks; and Marie's determination to pursue her goal in the field of nuclear physics even when it was clearly devastating her body with radiation sickness.

One thing is abundantly clear, namely, that millions of people owe their lives to the clear-headed sagacity, selfless devotion and remarkable scientific expertise of three outstanding people. Perhaps yet again we have examples of God's willingness to select his servants from all walks of life, even from beyond the formal precincts of the church and synagogue in order to bring health and relief to suffering humanity. As Jesus indicated, they (as we ourselves) shall be known by their fruit (Matthew 7:18–20).

We now turn our attention towards that intellectual giant Charles Darwin (1809–82). He was by profession a naturalist and a pioneer of experimental biology, with the rare gift of being able to draw together the disparate thoughts and ideas of others and form them into meaningful theories. His all-consuming passion was the ascent of the human species and the phylogenic course that this had taken. In 1831 armed with the rudiments of his theory of evolution he set sail round the world. He spent time on the Galapagos Islands observing the habits of finches and turtles and on returning home in 1836 was to spend almost another twenty years collecting material for his *On the Origin of Species by Means of Natural Selection*. On publication, the book caused a furore in Victorian England, and was labelled as blasphemous by some clerics, but was generally well accepted by biologists. In his book he argued that 'the evolution of present day morphology had been built up by gradual and opportunistic mechanism of natural selection'.

In 1871 he published *The Descent of Man and Selection in Relation to Sex*. From this it could be deduced that Man was not (only) just a little lower than the angels, he was at one with the subhuman animal world, even although he might choose to regard himself as a pinnacle (Rhodes 1985). This formed the basis for experimental biology. Man after all was just as physical, chemical and biological as his predecessors.

At about the same time as Darwin was engaged on his theory of evolution, another remarkable achievement was taking place in the hands of the Austrian monk, Gregor Johann Mendel (1822–84). Through his work and observations on cross-breeding round peas and wrinkled peas he was able to supply the missing links in Darwin's theory. From his observations, Mendel correctly deduced that by crossing round and wrinkled peas, he was able to show how variations occurred in individuals of the same species. The roundness he described as the 'dominant' character, and the wrinkled as the 'recessive' character. Mendel allowed the seeds of the rounded and wrinkled plants to pollinate themselves, and after repeated cross-pollinations observed that the dominant round peas oustripped the recessive wrinkled peas in the ratio of approximately three to one. Thus after thousands of experiments he formulated the basis from which natural selection proceeds to ensure the survival of the fittest.

Unknown to Mendel, he had stumbled on and laid the foundations of modern genetics, and his 'dominant' and 'recessive' characters were in time to become dominant and recessive genes. For a time his philosophy was known as Mendelism. He published his work in 1865, but because he did not realise its importance, his observations were to remain hidden in the archives until 1900.

As we have seen, this work complemented Darwin's theory of evolution and gives credence to our earlier observations on how, genetically speaking, Homosapiens sapiens, the pinnacle of creation, had triumphed over H. Cro-Magnon and H. neanderthalensis. Nowhere is this better stated than in the creation story as it is written in the book of Genesis (1:26). We borrow from the allegorical narrative: then God said 'and now we shall make human beings, they will be like us and resemble us'. This statement indicates, among other things, that the evolution of humankind had reached its evolutionary peak. The narrative continues: 'God looked at everything he had made, and he was very pleased' (Genesis 1:31). Pleased because the dominant feature was a perfection that reflected his own likeness and remained so until the Fall.

I do not know if any genetic implications were involved with Homosapiens sapiens at the Fall, although it does seem likely that some were. What does become clear is that the resultant recessive characteristics of humankind grow more evident as the human species succumbed to sickness and disease.

These recessive characteristics remained a feature of human life and suffering until God sent his Son to be the propitiation for our sins. Herein lies our hope, for through the atonement of Jesus Christ there is spiritual resurrection, and with this the recessive characteristics of human nature are changed by the dominant features of love and salvation. Alas, with most of us these dominant features will not be fully realised until we experience that great and final healing that takes place beyond the grave.

Returning to more basic things, it becomes easier to see how God, with the help of his servants, is enabling us to overcome disease and affliction. Mendel was indeed such a servant. He epitomised achievement in the finest possible way by successfully bridging the gap between science and religion. With him, on the one hand we have an Augustinian monk (later abbot) by vocation, and on the other an eminent scientist who laid the foundations for present-day genetics. We could not ask for better proof that science and religion are not only compatible, but that they are also capable of working together in perfect harmony.

The discoveries of Darwin and Mendel have had far-reaching effects upon society in general. Since the beginning of this century scientists have been endeavouring to unravel the precise course of human evolution, and geneticists have been trying to understand the minute details of hereditary variation. More recently anthropologists have been studying the interactions between humankind and the environment in an attempt to establish a genetic connection. Broadly speaking this whole specialist field comes under the heading of human ecology. Ecologists, as we know, are concerned with the environment and its effect upon the human species. In this day and age, perhaps a greater emphasis should be placed upon the effects that the human species is having upon the environment.

In its basic and fundamental form human ecology deals with nutritional requirements, and how humanity copes culturally and biologically with disease and other hazards in the environment.

Nineteenth-century Western society was swamped with cultural and biological hazards. Wars were being fought on many fronts with regular monotony; poverty and slum dwellings were for most the order of the day; health care where it existed was inadequate and often in the hands of unqualified people. Disease was rife, and many of the serious infections like typhoid, smallpox, tuberculosis, dysentery and a host of others were endemic. Apart from the discovery by Edward Jenner (1749–1823) of a vaccination against smallpox in 1798, little was done to alter this cultural and biological impasse. The science of microbiology was yet to be discovered.

At this point our attention is directed towards the young French chemist, Louis Pasteur (1822–95). Pasteur was engaged in the study of fermentation, with particular emphasis on the chemistry of life. This led him to turn his research towards human and animal pathogens, which subsequently enabled him to lay the foundations for the study of bacteriology, infectious diseases and immunology. His name is linked with the process of pasteurisation, particularly of milk, where through heating milk to 60 degrees Celsius for thirty minutes, pathogenic bacteria are killed and the development of other bacterial forms are delayed. He was a prolific writer and influenced many people, including the German bacteriologist Robert Koch (1843–1910).

Koch was noted for his work on anthrax, a fatal disease in animals. He perfected numerous bacteriological techniques for staining and fixing specimens, many of which are in use to this day. His greatest achievement was the isolation in 1882 of the tubercle bacillus, the organism responsible for producing tuberculosis in humans and other animals. He also carried out notable work on cholera and certain diseases affecting animals. He saw the importance of sterilisation and the need for identifying specific micro-organisms for specific diseases. He postulated that identifiable micro-organisms had to be shown to be capable of reproducing particular diseases in laboratory animals before a proper diagnosis could be made. In all he was a veritable giant among a select few who helped form the basis of microbiology and immunology.

At this time, the Russian Ilya Mechnikov (1845–1916) did valuable work on white blood cells in relation to infection. He demonstrated that some micro-organisms were capable of producing toxins such as the diphtheria bacterium and that the body responds by producing anti-toxins. This reaction is known as humoral or chemical resistance and is nowadays closely linked with transplant surgery and the perils of tissue rejection.

Throughout history humankind has constantly striven to conquer the environment. Often the struggle has been made worse by bigotry and contention. We notice it at the beginning with the Israelites, as they rebelled against Yahweh. We notice it again and again with the passage of time, as the struggle against cultural hazards such as poverty and injustice is further complicated by intolerance and indifference. Throughout all of this, biological hazards such as disease and infection were never far away. In spite of these ecological problems, it seems that when humankind is about to be overwhelmed, God steps in to bring relief and point the way to a richer and safer life.

We first perceive this when God sent Moses and the prophets to show the Israelites the error of their ways. We see it again in the example of Jesus who offered salvation as an alternative to sin and damnation. We see it with the church and her saints down the ages as they continue the work of Jesus. We see it with the men of science and technology as God uses them to unravel the mysteries of disease and infection. Finally, we see it with the men and women who strive to correct social injustice, and the educators who strive to bring knowledge and understanding.

Nineteenth-century England and Western society saw many advances in medical science and technology. Although the biological hazards were being challenged and overcome, some of the cultural hazards were still much in evidence. One of these was the appalling state of patient and nursing care in the hospitals, a situation not only confined to England, but which extended throughout the whole of the Western world. It is at this point that God sent the redoubtable Florence Nightingale (1820–1910).

Florence Nightingale was born into a prosperous family. Socially, she was well connected with the rich and powerful, an asset she was later able to exploit in her contacts with influential government ministers. Being a lady of substance, she was able to travel extensively. During a trip to Germany in 1850 she encountered Pastor Fliedner in Kaiseswerth. Fliedner had founded the Institution of Kaiserswerth on the Rhine for the training of church deaconesses. His methods and influence had spread to other institutions including infant and industrial schools, as well as a female penitentiary. All of this impressed itself upon Florence Nightingale who throughout her life showed a great interest in the care of the sick.

In 1853 she was appointed Superintendent to the Institution for the care of Sick Gentlewomen in Distressed Circumstances at a time when this institution was facing re-organisation. Florence Nightingale entered into the task with zeal and determination. One of her innovations was the introduction of call bells for the patients (Coleman 1985). She also stipulated that the acceptance of the gentlewomen should be on an interdenominational basis, in an attempt to remove religious barriers and intolerance. She further insisted upon the need for clean bed linen. This may seem to be a strange requirement, but in those days it was not uncommon for new patients to inherit the dirty and sometime soiled bed linen of previous incumbents. With her sense of perception she introduced a system of signed contracts with suppliers and wholesalers, and refused to accept goods which were not up to standard.

At that time Britain and its allies were at war with Russia. A correspondent with *The Times* newspaper delivered a censorious attack on the government condemning the appalling conditions under which sick and wounded soldiers were being tended in the Crimea with too few surgeons, no nurses and a lack of dressings.

The Secretary for War, Sidney Herbert, approached Florence Nightingale with the request that she go to Scutari and organise proper hospital facilities for the sick and wounded. She took with her a small group of nurses of mixed background and experience and set sail for the Crimea. This was to mark the turning point for nursing care and establish Florence Nightingale as the pioneer of nursing reform. She and her nurses had a miraculous effect upon the situation in Scutari and succeeded in reducing the death rate among patients from forty-two per cent to two per cent (Coleman 1985). She also removed the sense of hopelessness that was all too evident among the hospitalised soldiers, who were invariably resigned to their fate.

When she returned from the Crimea, Florence Nightingale was a national heroine. As a reward, she was given £50,000 to start the School of Nursing at St Thomas's Hospital in London. Her methods were revolutionary and extended beyond nursing care to take on the design of hospitals and the re-styling of wards along pavilion lines, with an emphasis on fresh air, cleanliness and light. She also recommended that hospital grounds be laid out with gardens to aid convalescence. Soon her fame extended to the rest of Europe and America, and her *Notes on Nursing* became compulsory reading for all nurses in training.

Other advances in medical practice were made with the discovery of antisepsis. The surgeon Jospeh Lister (1827–1912) was to lead the way in antiseptic surgery. Lister was greatly influenced by the discoveries of Pasteur and looked for practical ways to implement them and to overcome the bacterial hazards in his surgical practice. The result was the introduction of his famous carbolic spray with which he disinfected the site of operation. The results were dramatic in dealing with hospital infections following operations, and in dealing with hospital infections in general. Up until then, post-operative infections, which were considerable, were generally accepted as the norm, and airily dismissed by surgeons under the general appellation of 'laudable pus'!

The discovery of anaesthesia is also a further landmark. Anaesthetic gases like nitrous oxide and ether had been known for some time. Many of these agents were used as 'party frolics' by leading medical and dental men of the time, as a means of entertaining dinner guests, as well as on other social occasions. An American dentist, Horace Wells (1815–48) from Connecticut, was quick to realise its usefulness in the practice of dentistry, and persuaded a visiting chemistry lecturer to administer laughing gas on himself for the purpose of extracting a tooth. The operation was carried out painlessly. His partner William T. Morton (1819–68) was more adept in the use of ether, and administered it as an anaesthetic at the Massachusetts General Hospital in 1846 for the surgeon John Collins Warren (1778–1856). Again, the operation was carried out painlessly.

In Edinburgh, there were more party frolics with various anaesthetic agents. The obstetrician James Young Simpson (1811–70) was greatly impressed with the anaesthetic qualities of chloroform and decided to use it to combat pain in childbirth. Obstetrically, this was a great success, but news of its use caused a great uproar with the Scottish Kirk. The bible was quoted at Simpson by some of the clerics – 'In sorrow shalt thou bring forth' – and he was accused of going against nature. The row continued unabated until the revered sovereign, Queen Victoria, had two of her babies delivered under chloroform anaesthesia. Only then was chloroform made respectable; for a while afterwards it became known as 'chloroforme à la reine'.

With the advent of anaesthesia and the discoveries in bacteriology, surgery was made safer. By the end of the nineteenth century operations were being carried out for lesions in most parts of the body with the exception of the chest and the cranial cavities. Operations involving the latter did not become technically possible until well into the twentieth century (Rhodes 1985).

For some, the advent of these various discoveries may give the impression that their timing was haphazard, bearing no relationship to their importance. They appear little more than a series of egocentric happenings aimed at trying to satisfy humanity's insatiable quest for knowledge and understanding. On reflection, it can be seen that that was not the case, and that the timing of these discoveries was part of a carefully co-ordinated plan that God had chosen for our benefit. For example, what purpose would anaesthesia have served without the technical skills of the surgeon? And vice versa. Or, as in the case of surgical expertise, what use would an understanding of bacteriology have been without antiseptic agents to deal with those lethal antagonists? And, what use would any of these have been without proper nursing care? In fact, throughout, we see the hand of God at work, revealing the nature of disease and infection, and putting into the hands of humankind the means with which to deal with it. This is, after all, part of the ecological inheritance that humankind had brought upon itself as a result of the Fall, and which God in his mercy has helped us to conquer and overcome. Further, it is not a casual affair, where events and discoveries have happened willy-nilly, but part of a carefully planned revelation aimed at bringing relief to suffering humanity.

Further evidence of the ecological struggle is not difficult to see, particularly with the hazards of tropical diseases. Malaria, for example, was rife, often fatal, and had been the scourge of the East for hundreds of years. Many Eastern outposts were manned by doctors serving with the armed forces. Among these was Patrick Manson (1844–1922), a Scot working in Hong Kong. He made some interesting observations on blood taken from patients suffering from malaria, and later went on to found the London School of Tropical Medicine. Ronald Ross (1857–1932) through diligent scrutiny while serving in India showed the aetiological connection between the mosquito bite and the cycle of events which caused malaria, and thus ended the mystery.

At home the importance of public health and preventive medicine was brought to the attention of the government from an unlikely source, a Unitarian minister named Thomas Southwood-Smith (1788–1861), who published his observations in *The Philosophy of Health*. Later he was co-opted on to the General Board of Health, which was set up by the government of the time to monitor and protect the health of the nation.

All of these are further instances of the revelations that God had chosen to help humankind in its constant struggle against various aspects of human ecology, particularly disease.

Towards the end of the nineteenth century we encounter another intellectual genius in that controversial figure Sigmund Freud (1856–1939). Freud was born in Freiburg, in present-day Czechoslovakia, and had his medical training in Vienna. On receiving his doctorate he began by specialising in neurology, but on taking up a new appointment at the Salpêtrière Hospital in Paris he quickly came under the influence of Jean-Martin Charcot, and just as quickly transferred his attention to the speciality of psycho-analysis. His knowledge of anatomy and in particular neuro-anatomy gave him an advantage over his peers. He was able to bring together a lot of loosely held ideas and theories of the time and form a proper basis for nineteenth-century psycho-analysis. He was an outspoken advocate of psychological medicine. His extreme views did not always endear him to his friends and colleagues. His theory of pansexuality, whereby he attributed all psychological problems to repressed sexual desire, caused an outcry. Freud responded by putting up his consultation fees (Coleman 1985). Sadly, this genius tends to be remembered more for his extravagant claims than for the fact that he laid the foundation for nineteenth-century psycho-analysis and twentieth-century psychiatry.

We come to the end of this momentous period – the nineteenth century. Never before or since have we known such a concentration of intellectual giants, by whose ideas, theories and philosophies God was able to release and give to humanity the revelations that were to inspire twentieth-century medical thinking.

As a rule, humankind tends to think in a confined and restricted way, assuming that God works only through those who are specifically committed to him or ordained into the priesthood or religious life. But the examples amassed above show that the Lord of history can and does use whomever he chooses to achieve his purpose and bring relief to suffering humanity, in the same way as he works through many people and circumstances to bring people to faith in his Son (The Word Amongst Us 1991).

8

The limitations of early twentieth-century medicine

Paradoxically, the standard of medical care and medical training in Western society at the beginning of the twentieth century left much to be desired, especially when compared with the heady achievements of the previous century. It is as though the enlightenment of nineteenth-century scientific development had suddenly become eclipsed, and the harsh reality of disease and infection held dominance over the lives of the people. The Boer War was being fought and it is here that we start. Large sections of the British Army were invalided home, not because of wounds or injuries, but simply because they were medically and dentally unfit. This sent the alarm bells ringing throughout Whitehall, because it was suddenly realised that the security of the nation depended upon the fitness of its people, and this lack of fitness was all too apparent.

Doctors at that time were little more than diagnosticians and prognosticians whose therapeutic remedies were sadly deficient and at times quite useless. The drugs that were available consisted mainly of opium and its derivatives, digitalis, a few metallic salts, bismuth, counter-irritants to rub on the skin, stimulants, sedatives and a few herbal remedies in the form of linctuses and tinctures; a not very formidable list to stem the flow of disease and infection, especially when it is considered that the prognosis for any one of a list of complaints was poor and usually fatal.

Medical training varied from country to country. In the United

Kingdom the standard of medical training was fairly basic. The various licensing bodies that controlled the practice of medicine were situated in Edinburgh, Glasgow and London. These licensing authorities enabled practitioners to practise but only in designated areas. Legislation governing the practice of medicine was based on various Medical Acts beginning with the Medical Act of 1858 which has since been revised and updated, as in the Medical Acts of 1950 and 1983. All of this now comes under the aegis of the General Medical Council which is the body responsible for medical education, registration and disciplinary procedures. A similar organisation, the General Dental Council, exists for dental education, registration and disciplinary procedures.

Corresponding arrangements obtain for most other countries in the Western world, but this was not always the case. For example, in the United States of America at the beginning of the century, medical training varied from state to state, and in the worst of these it was possible often to receive a medical qualification after only two years' training, and in some instances without even having seen a sick patient (Coleman 1985). The greatest step forward in American medical training and medical care was due to the Quaker philanthropist Johns Hopkins (1795–1873), who bequeathed large sums of money for the founding of a medical school which today still bears his name. By the beginning of the twentieth century these benefits were starting to be felt and soon spread to other states causing them to elevate their standards of medical training and practice.

Back in the United Kingdom, the alarm bells were still ringing, and in 1911 the Welsh politician Lloyd George as Chancellor of the Exchequer introduced a national health insurance scheme, copied from Germany, which included sickness benefit and an old-age pension. He also initiated the school medical and dental services to monitor child health and offer treatment wherever it was found to be necessary. At last it was being realised that the health of the nation begins with its child population. A system of health visitors was introduced, whose job it was to instruct nursing and expectant mothers in the home on matters of hygiene and health care. At this point we see the emphasis on health care shifting from curative medical practice to that of preventive medical care, even although the preventive measures were embryonic and the curative measures still left much to be desired.

The adage that 'prevention is better than cure' is true for all ages. We see it first demonstrated during the time of the Israelites with the introduction of their teaching on health. At times the commonsense values of this adage have been lost, to return again usually as a result of trial and error. One does not know what prompted Edward Jenner, in the eighteenth century, to observe that milkmaids acquired immunity against smallpox simply through receiving attenuated doses of cowpox toxins; but he was quick to realise that the immunity acquired by the milkmaids could also be made available to the populace at large. This formed the basis for twentieth-century immunisation against other infectious diseases, and emphasised again that prevention is better than cure. It also secured a place for that speciality that we now call preventive medicine.

During the first half of the twentieth century there were few remedies for the all-too-common infectious diseases. You would very likely have died if you had developed pneumonia, puerperal fever, meningitis, dysentery, typhoid, diphtheria or tuberculosis. Blood poisoning was also invariably fatal, and syphilis and gonorrhoea were lifelong tragedies for both the patient and his or her family. The emphasis had to be on prevention and public health experts set about discovering immunising programmes that would give protection. This emphasis on prevention has now produced safeguards against many of the infectious diseases, although we had to wait until after the Second World War before successful trials produced protection against poliomyelitis and tuberculosis.

During this time there were no earth-shattering changes in the realms of curative medicine. Paul Ehrlich (1854–1915), the German bacteriologist and physician, dreamt of a 'magic bullet' that would cure all disease. He is noted for his work on immunology, but his greatest contribution was to the discovery of salvarsan – an arsenical compound for the treatment of syphilis. Ehrlich is also credited with being the founder of that area of medical science known as chemotherapy. Sadly he died before the introduction of antibiotics and did not see his dream of a 'magic bullet' realised.

Working at St Mary's Hospital in London, the bacteriologist Alexander Fleming (1881–1955) noticed that some of his culture plates containing staphylococcus microbes had become accidentally contaminated with a mould which he later identified as Penicillium notatum. The active substance in the mould (penicillin) had the capability of dissolving the colony of staphylococcus. Further experiments proved that penicillin was non-toxic to animals even when given in large doses. This was to prove a considerable advantage over the sulpha drugs.

Like so many outstanding achievements, Fleming's results were to lie hidden for another ten years or so before their real value was appreciated. The importance of his work was to a large extent overshadowed by the advent of the sulpha drugs, which were then mistaken for Ehrlich's 'magic bullet'. Unfortunately, the use of these drugs, although life saving for many, including Winston Churchill, could cause serious side-effects by way of kidney damage and certain blood diseases.

The approach of the Second World War then caused scientists to take another look at Fleming's discovery. The result was the purifying and synthesising of penicillin by Howard Florey and Ernest Chain, and the arrival of a wide range of antibiotics which were to put paid to a host of infectious diseases such as tuberculosis, meningitis and syphilis and a large number of common infections and septic conditions that had barely been controlled by conventional methods.

Humankind was slowly but surely conquering that ecological factor which in the past had greatly reduced life expectancy. Medical science was now capable of improving the quality of life by curing diseases which before had always proved fatal. Surgical expertise and new procedures were also playing their part in improving and raising the expectations of the chronically sick patient, as well as dealing more efficiently with acute and minor ailments, so that by the closing decades of the twentieth century, organ transplants and replacement joints have now become commonplace.

As we approach the end of the present century there is no shortage of technological know-how and expertise. As with life expectancy, the quality of life for most, especially in Western society, has now been vastly improved. The age-old dichotomy between science and religion, although not entirely mended, is now less apparent. One element in the advance of medical science is that those in the vanguard are willing to concede that the healing of people's souls does much to assist in the healing of their bodies and minds. Medical people are also now less opposed to what is called alternative medicine. This term includes those areas of healing that are non-scientific and which are often related to faith and prayer – for example, the phenomenon of Lourdes where carefully documented and authenticated cures have occurred, usually after all other remedies have failed.

Although the advances in medical science have been many and great, the battle against disease and suffering continues. A recent consultative document issued in 1991 by the British Government on 'The Health of the Nation' shows that coronary heart disease and strokes account for twelve per cent of all deaths and five per cent of deaths under sixty-five years; cancers account for twenty-five per cent of deaths; smoking is the largest single preventable cause of death; and HIV/Aids (Acquired Immune Deficiency Syndrome) is the greatest new threat to public health in this century. We also learn from the same statistics that twenty per cent of the total National Health Service funding is spent on mental health.

Compelling and revealing these statistics might be, but they are as nothing compared with the statistics that separate Western society from the developing nations of the third world, where access to basic medical care, where present, is minimal; where survival is on a day-to-day basis dependent on international aid programmes; where millions of people face famine and deprivation on a scale never before envisaged; and where the problem of refugees grows daily. These are some of the problems that have arisen from this new divide, but they are not peculiar to the developing nations. Western society also has its divisions where the rich get richer and the poor get poorer, and where all the major towns and cities have their unacceptable levels of homelessness and poverty. In the centre of London, an estimated one thousand people sleep under cardboard boxes every night. Bad as these statistics might be, they are only the tip of the iceberg, and symptomatic of an ailing society.

A large proportion of people who attend their doctor or hospital have no physical illness at all. A British press article of June 1991, replying to the Government's document on 'The Health of the Nation' stated that these patients '. . . suffer from complaints that (the doctor) can only call, for lack of a better term, existential' (Daniels, *The Daily Telegraph*, June 1991). This same doctor goes on to say that their chief complaint is boredom coupled with a vague and deep resentment that gnaws at the heart. In many cases their lives are governed by a continuous diet of television and soap operas – a life of make-believe that breeds passivity and robs life of all true meaning and purpose.

9

Suffering and the challenge of Jesus

We could be excused for asking ourselves: what has gone wrong? Are the symptoms I have discussed part of a continuous process where human nature is in constant travail? For it seems that there is no escape from the relentless punishment that society inflicts upon itself. Much of our suffering, like the first apostasy, is of our own doing.

Returning to that first apostasy – what do we see? We see a race that had lost its integrity, virtue and innocence and had inherited a proclivity to sin. That proclivity to sin is still present and all around us; but this need not be the case. God loves each one of us and has demonstrated that love from the moment the theologians refer to as the Fall – and even before that – right up until now. We get glimpses of this love through the prophets:

> Israel, you are like a young wife, deserted by her husband and deeply distressed. But the Lord calls you back to him and says; 'For one brief moment I left you; with deep love I will take you back.
> I turned away angry for only a moment, but I will show you my love for ever'
> So says the Lord who saves you.
> (Isaiah 54:6–8).

We see further evidence of God's love being repeated down the ages, and one of the ways that he has shown his love is by helping us to conquer the disease in our environment. The various discoveries that medical science has made in all ages, these momentous revelations, are no chance happenings, but part of the divine plan aimed at helping humankind to conquer the self-imposed hazards caused by the Fall.

But there is more to life than health of body and mind, important as that might be. This is one of the reasons why God sent his Son into the world. With Jesus, we have the perfect example, the blueprint, for living out our human existence. Yet he is more than just an example, he is the propitiation for our sins. However, we cannot just pay lip service to this truth. We have to be willing to die with Jesus to sin, and we do this through our Christian baptism. If we die with Jesus and allow our sins to be crucified with him, then we must surely rise with him to a new life, a life 'through him, with him, (and) in him . . .', as the priest says in the final doxology at the Mass.

Most of us are baptised in infancy and someone else takes these vows on our behalf, but sooner or later the reality of their importance has to be faced if we intend to live out the Christian life. When that reality is fully accepted, we are able to take the next step and receive the challenge of the beatitudes and the sermon on the mount, both of which sum up the teachings of Jesus. Both appeal to a universal longing of the human heart, and promise a satisfaction of soul which can be found only in obedience to that ethical code summed up in the Commandments, where Jesus himself proclaimed, 'Do not think that I have come to do away with the Law of Moses and the teachings of the prophets. I have not come to do away with them, but to make their teachings come true' (Matthew 5:17).

It is one thing to accept the teachings of Jesus, but another thing to put them into practice. Even the disciples realised this basic truth when they asked Jesus to teach them to pray. It was at that point that Jesus gave them the Lord's prayer, but more than that he was helping them to make contact with his Father and their Father. Without this contact with the Father, made available through Jesus (Matthew 6:9–13; 23:9), the teachings of Jesus are but objects of meditation and not capable of being understood, let alone being implemented. Prayer then is our lifeline; a fact that

Jesus himself demonstrated by his own need to take himself away from the others (Mark 1:35) in order to spend time with his Father.

For the Christian the authority of the Gospels is absolute touching on the duty of prayer, although for recent believers there might be some sort of intellectual conflict, simply because the results of prayer cannot be proved scientifically. For obvious reasons this proof is not available since faith is an essential part of the prayer process, and proof would simply destroy that faith. Let it therefore suffice to say that the practice of prayer by countless races of humankind throughout many generations is not likely to be based upon sheer delusion. Millions of people, including many talented and gifted souls, have prayed and continue to pray because experience has taught them that prayer is efficacious.

Conerning places, times and attitudes towards prayer, little is to be found in the scriptures. For the Jew during biblical times, the chief place was the temple – 'My Temple will be called a house of prayer' (Matthew 21:13); (Mark 11:17); (Luke 19:46). We find also that not much is said about the times of prayer, but we read that Jesus rose before daylight and went to a lonely place to pray (Mark 1:35); and of his continuing all night in prayer before he chose the twelve (Luke 6:12). The evening before he was arrested he again spent in prayer.

The standing posture for prayer was common among the Jews. Catholics to this day continue this practice although less rigidly. But in the garden, Jesus knelt on that fateful night (Luke 22:41). Perhaps from this example early Christians as well as many others down the ages have adopted the kneeling posture.

Much more important, though, than places, times and postures for prayer is the fact that Jesus by his own example has taught us the importance of prayer. Jesus prayed not just to set us an example, but in order that he might fulfil all righteousness, thereby submitting to the will of his Father. His example in every sense is truly remarkable; if in a life such as his there was not only time but the need for prayer, how very much more must there be time and need for prayer in lives like ours.

Jesus's prayers were not always for others. In most cases we do not know why Jesus prayed, but have to deduce the reason from the context of what was happening at the time. On the occasion in the garden before his passion, we know that he prayed for himself (Matthew 26:39); (Mark 14:35); (Luke 22:41). Shortly after this and following the Last Supper, we know that he prayed for the disciples (John 17:20–26), and for the whole church (John 17:6–19), and a few hours later he prayed for those who crucified him (Luke 23:34). We have a remarkable series of examples of intercession not only for groups of people, large and small, but also for an individual, when he assured Peter that he had prayed for him, that his faith would not fail (Luke 22:32).

From this we see something of the importance that Jesus attached to prayer and something of the importance that we should attach to prayer. Prayer is our lifeline if we intend to live out the Christian life. It is the means by which we re-charge our spiritual batteries.

10

Prayer – especially contemplative prayer

Generally speaking, there are three distinct forms of prayer. There is vocal prayer, meditative prayer and contemplative prayer.

Vocal prayer is a prayer of the lips which may be said or sung. It is the type of prayer with which most of us are familiar, and which is used either singularly for private devotions or for gatherings large or small. In vocal prayers there are many pre-formed prayers and verses where the words and the language are most beautiful and which inspire the soul with thoughts of love and adoration. Here we have words which sum up our innermost feelings and express the yearnings of the soul.

In meditative prayer the lips are silent and the mind is active. With this form of prayer, the prayer is centred in the mind as a phrase or picture which meditates on God the Father and his goodness; or it may be a piece of scripture or some other holy work. The mind seeks to discover fresh understanding and insight by deliberating on the particular phrase or picture. With practice this form of prayer becomes more and more God-centred.

Finally, we come to contemplative prayer where the lips and the mind are quiet, and where the heart will reach out to God and concentrate upon his presence in our innermost being. Contemplative prayer is not new, it was the prayer of the early church and has been greatly used by the saints of all ages, and in particular the medieval saints. Then it fell into disuse largely because it was mistakenly confused with Quietism – a poor substitute which consists of making a once-and-for-all act of love for God, with the intention of never bringing to mind the original act of surrender (Borst 1979). Quietism is a prayer more of the will and tends to centre around a form of stoicism, which never could really be considered as a substitute for the prayers of the contemplative.

Contemplative prayer is a gift from God that allows the soul to commune with its Maker in a most loving and intimate way, a gift that causes the heart and the will to yearn for the divine presence that lies within each one of us. 'By love he can be touched and embraced, never by thought': so said the author of *The Cloud of Unknowing* (chapter 6).

This then explains the embrace which binds the soul with its redeemer as it contemplates the divine presence within. It is an act of love; no process of thought is involved. It is a gift from God.

Many have found that the contemplative attitude to prayer gives not only a greater awareness of God's presence but enables them to practise his presence not only in the intimate moments of 'quiet' but also as a rule of life. St Teresa of Avila (1515–82) calls it the prayer of recollection (Hamilton 1963), while her confidant and helper St John of the Cross says 'Contemplation is nothing else but a secret, peaceful infusion of God, which, if admitted, will set the soul on fire with the spirit of love' (Borst 1979).

The Trappist monk Thomas Merton (1915–68), whose prose writings gave a contemporary interpretation of the contemplative life and whose forty books and innumerable essays explored every aspect of contemplative prayer, had a profound effect upon his own generation and in particular his contemporaries of the 1950s and 1960s.

Another modern advocate of the contemplative attitude to prayer was Pope John XXIII (1881–1963). In his encyclical letter 'Pacem in Terris' he explores the signs and the needs of the times, and in doing this reveals the contemplative attitude upon which his own life was rooted. An extract from 'Pacem in Terris' instructs us:

Every believer in this world of ours must be a spark of light, a centre of love; a vivifying leaven amidst his fellow men. But he will be this all the more perfectly, the more closely he lives in communion with God in the intimacy of his own soul.

(Borst 1979)

Last but by no means least, Sister Briege McKenna, joint author of *Miracles do Happen*, and herself miraculously healed of severe rheumatic disease combines a remarkable healing ministry with her devotion to contemplative prayer. Her profound words in *Miracles do Happen* and in her numerous talks have given encouragement and a new dimension to the spiritual lives of many.

Contemplative prayer is not a prayer that has been reserved only for a select few among the great and illustrious in the priesthood or the religious life. In the Old Testament it was the prayer of the prophets and the Jewish people as they stood before the Ark of the Covenant seeking the face of Yahweh during their wanderings in the wilderness, and later when the Ark was permanently installed in the temple at Jerusalem. It was through contemplation, when they were not rebelling and seeking to do their own will, that they offered their love and obedience to the God of Irsael and sought his will through the prophets and elders.

Then we have the supreme example of Jesus contemplating his heavenly Father in the desert place and on the mountainside. Like us the human part of Jesus needed to know the will of his Father, and this he did in solitude, by fasting and by watching in prayer, all the time contemplating the divine presence of his heavenly Father. Jesus offers us this same precious opportunity to re-enact the experience of prayer that he himself had with his Father in the quietness of our own heart. That same contemplative experience can actually be ours, and is there for the asking; so that we too can be in him, just as he is in us. We *can* experience this intimate union with our living Lord, but we have to be willing to ask for the gift of contemplation, for gift it is.

Through contemplation we come face to face, as it were, with our Lord in the depth and quietness of our souls. If we have a genuine interest in and need for contemplative prayer then we need only ask for this special gift; but we should not enter lightly upon this undertaking. Contemplative prayer calls for commitment and a willingness to set aside a given time and place – from half an hour to an hour each day at least.

Having asked for the gift, then believe that you have received it (Luke 11:13) (Matthew 7:7–11).

Here are a few guide lines that we might find useful. As we grow into the practice these can be modified to suit our own particular need.

In vocal prayer as in meditative prayer we begin by expressing our love and gratitude, and offering praise to God the Father, his Son and the Holy Spirit. This simple act of devotion helps create a right attitude and makes prayer more conducive. The same is true for contemplative prayer. Having created the right attitude, we can then put into practice the following stages which will enable us to become immersed in the prayer of contemplation. A useful mnemonic is the made-up word R A S A R . The letters of the word help us to remember each stage. As with all prayer, the Holy Spirit is there to help us; so we begin by asking the Holy Spirit to help us to relax:

R stands for *relaxation*. One should not be too reticent about approaching the Holy Spirit for help, for often the Holy Spirit is the most neglected person of the Trinity. We do well therefore to let this third person share in our prayers and to ask for his help in creating this relaxed attitude.

A stands for the willingness to *acknowledge* the presence of the Holy Spirit within us. The gift of the Holy Spirit is the normal accompaniment of our Christian baptism. Even if he exists only in his latent form within our baptised soul, he is anxious that we should acknowledge his presence. At this point it is not out of place to ask for a greater awareness of his presence.

S stands for *submission* or *surrender*. The submission of our will to the will of the Holy Spirit, an act of *surrender*. Again it may be necessary to ask the Spirit to help us make this commitment.

A stands for *acceptance* and the willingness to accept whatever God the Father and his Son Jesus have chosen for us; in other words, a conscious effort to accept God's will instead of our own, a willingness to give up our possessiveness in order that we might be possessed by him.

R stands for *repentance* for all our sins past and present. Here it is important that we should not be over-scrupulous and preoccupied with the minutiae of past sins. It is enough that we recognise our unworthiness and leave the rest to God. Also under this heading R leads on to the stage of *reconciliation* when we ask to be reconciled to the Father through his Son, strong in the knowledge that our sins are forgiven. If at this stage we find it difficult to believe that our sins have been forgiven, then there is nothing to prevent us asking Jesus for the grace to accept his forgiveness and again leave the rest to him. 'Lord I believe, help thou my unbelief' is a useful prayer when uttered with sincerity.

We may feel that we wish to make certain petitions at this juncture. This we should do but the emphasis is on contemplation where the lips and the mind are at rest. The contemplative attitude can be greatly assisted at this point by repeating the prayer to Jesus: 'Lord Jesus Christ, Son of God, have mercy on me a sinner'.

We should repeat this prayer over and over again in a gentle rhythmical way until we are able to contemplate that inner peace, 'the peace that passeth all understanding'. We can help maintain this peace or awareness of the divine presence by repeating the prayer or just by uttering his name, 'Jesus'. To begin with we may find this part difficult, and we may have to adopt an attitude of perseverance, but our commitment will be rewarded.

We should not confine our contemplative prayers to that time of the day reserved for our 'quiet' time. It is a worthwhile habit to repeat the Jesus prayer at various times throughout the day either in times of crisis or even just as we go about our daily business.

11

Suffering and the contemplative

We have examined prayer in general, and contemplative prayer in particular. We now turn our attention to that other part of the dual partnership that appears in the title: suffering.

Suffering is something that, as we have seen, is peculiar to our human existence. It affects our physical and psychical faculties, as well as our spiritual lives. It touches us all differently depending on our circumstances and our threshold to tolerate its presence. Depending on this threshold and depending on our personality it can either ennoble or embitter. It can rarely be viewed with indifference. Jesus was all too familiar with its presence and came to destroy the evil that perpetuates its presence in our lives.

We turn to Jesus because the suffering of our Lord was no mere chance happening, it was pre-ordained. We who are joined to Christ by our baptism and are committed to the Christian life must also expect to suffer. Such are the consequences of that first apostasy when humanity excluded itself from the original plan and purpose that God had chosen for it. Much of the New Testament is devoted to this sombre aspect of Christian life, where suffering is expounded in every sense but often in an attempt to elucidate the suffering experienced by Jesus in his earthly ministry, and the part that this was to play in our salvation.

We misunderstand Christ's donning of our human form if we confine his suffering to the agony of the cross. The bitter experience of the events of that last week, which culminated in the crucifixion, were typical of his life throughout. The emptying of himself in order that he might become the partner of humanity to atone for our sins, and his unrelenting struggle against sin for righteousness' sake, were in fact suffering at its worst. In many ways the agony of the garden and the terrors of the cross were but the final outrage in the drama of his humiliation.

To emphasise this point, we should not allow the intensity of his physical agony to obscure his spiritual woes. How great must have been his grief when his sinless soul was confronted with selfishness, disobedience, hard-heartedness, unresponsiveness and unrepentant sin in all its guises. Indeed this was 'a man of sorrows, and acquainted with grief' (Isaiah 53:3). By donning our flesh Jesus exposed the enormity of sin. Arrayed against him were the fearful extremes to which sin and evil were prepared to go to overcome goodness.

As we have seen we too do not escape the experiences that came to him (John 15:20), even if these should be considerably less than his. However, it would be a mistake to deduce from the teachings of Jesus that suffering on our part was the one, all-important pre-condition of *future* happiness.

Our Christian faith is a religion of *present* happiness, and joy is a *present* fruit of the spirit (Galatians 5:22). The Kingdom of God *present* among us is peace and joy (Romans 14:17). Christianity is full of paradoxes and one of these is that happiness can coexist with sorrow. Jesus himself, 'the man of sorrows', was not an unhappy man. He radiated joy, happiness and a spirit of serenity. In the beatitudes Jesus revealed the secret of this happiness, when he said 'happy are those who are persecuted because they do what God requires; the kingdom of heaven belongs to them!' (Matthew 5:10).

Sorrowful, yet always rejoicing (2 Corinthians 6:10) this is the paradox of New Testament teaching and the fundamental truth which some individuals fail to recognise when they seek perpetual happiness, and become sadly disillusioned when all does not go well.

Jesus had no illusions about suffering, and knew only too well its consequences in his own life. As we have seen, Jesus recognised suffering for what it was and came to destroy the evil that caused it, sin.

In spite of the sorrow and grief which suffering engenders, there is a paradox here which brings with it the peace which passeth all understanding, and the joy which comes in union with Christ. Victory lies with this peace and this joy. Herein is the triumph of Jesus which enabled him to conquer suffering and death, the triumph which enabled St Paul to say in his second letter to the Corinthians 'sorrowful, yet always rejoicing', when he described his own state and that of his fellow Christians. It is this which enabled St Paul, in the end, to bear his thorn in the flesh with complete indifference, and wear the martyr's crown with equanimity, 'for it is when I am weak that I am strong' (2 Corinthians 12:10).

It is with this same grace that the martyrs in all ages have accepted the challenge of their supreme sacrifice, and this which has also enabled others to suffer the slings and arrows which were often a consequence of witnessing for their Lord.

O death, where is thy sting?
O grave, where is thy victory?
(1 Corinthians 15:55)

12

Conclusions

We have examined closely human suffering in all ages through the history of medical care. We have examined the suffering of our Lord in a fair amount of detail. We have discovered that human suffering is not much altered in the twentieth century from the suffering of earlier times, except of course that we in the twentieth century have more sophisticated ways of dealing with it. Our focus on the suffering of Jesus is important because it is with Jesus that we have the means and the grace to deal with it. This does not mean that we should ignore the advantages and discoveries of medical science, for these also come from God, even although humankind may tend to think that it is humanity's wisdom that has produced them. It is only through God's revelations that humankind has been able to use its ingenuity to bring to light that which God has revealed in the first place. This is further evidence of God's love, where after the first apostasy he promised to show humankind how to deal with and come to terms with that part of human ecology, disease and suffering.

A further bonus is of course the sacrifice of Jesus who himself became the propitiation for our sins and our suffering. Jesus does not say that we will not have suffering but does show us how to deal with it, even if it means going to the doctor or the dentist. Further, when we reach the limitations of medical science, Jesus does not shrug his shoulders and say that nothing can be done. As with all suffering, be it physical, psychological or spiritual, his words are always appropriate: 'Come unto me all ye that labour [and suffer] and I will give you rest'.

We can come unto Jesus in many ways, but all the more perfectly if we have the gift of being able to contemplate his divine presence within our souls. Here we can find him, not by thinking about him but by loving and yearning for him. Therefore ask for this gift, if you have not already received it, and learn to contemplate his presence in the quietness of your heart, and write down the thoughts he will give you. You will be surprised at what he will reveal to you through this form of guidance. Thus we can meet our risen Lord face to face. Thus we can listen to his voice, a gentle voice not heard with physical ears, but heard only within the depths of our soul. This is where Jesus allows our spirit to become one with his spirit. This is contemplation. This is the life that Jesus has promised for those that believe in him and love him. This is where we can cast off the burden of pain and suffering even when it persists after the limitations of medical science have been reached. If like St Paul we have been asked to bear our 'thorn in the flesh', then it is here in the depths of our soul that we will be given the grace to do so.

Unlike St Paul, we are not always asked to bear with our suffering. Most of us can seek the help and relief that God has provided for our use through medicine and surgery and other aids. I would add that the days of the healing miracles are not over and there is plenty of evidence to show that these still continue. Sadly, we do not always take advantage of the Church's healing ministry. In the letter from St James (5:14) we are expressly invited to 'send for the church elders, who will pray for [the sick person] and rub olive-oil on him [or her] in the name of the Lord. . .' This does not mean of course that we should do this to the exclusion of medical science, but rather in conjunction with it, for each complements the other. We know that there are occasions when doctors do not have the answer to our maladies and that prayer is often our only hope, and we trust that this should be, for miracles do happen. So remarked Sister Briege McKenna as she was miraculously and spontaneously healed of severe arthritis at her convent at Tampa in Florida in December 1970. She herself, using Jesus's healing gift, has brought similar miraculous healings to many others.

Recently I met a young lady who has a remarkable healing gift.

Her name is Dinah. She explains quite simply that her healing gift comes from God. She employs the laying-on of hands in conjunction with the relaxation techniques used in yoga. To use her own words, 'I simply plug into the Almighty and allow his healing grace to flow through me like "electricity" to the person being healed'. This healing grace manifests itself in the form of heat, and gives healing and comfort to those in need. I know of several successes where Dinah has been used as an instrument of healing.

Other instances of recorded and unrecorded healing miracles are known to happen all the time among the faithful, in homes and churches and even over the telephone. Many of the recorded miracles have taken place at the various Marian shrines, in particular Lourdes. The following two instances are taken from a host of authentic cures listed at the Bureau des Constatations Médicales de Lourdes.

1 The healing on 26 September 1947 of a boy who was blind because of optic atrophy and chorioretinitis. The spontaneous healing occurred following a visit to the Stations of the Cross. Afterwards he was bathed in the baths. His cure became evident when he commented to his mother on the beauty of the stained glass windows at the baths, and later when he stooped to pick up a piece of wood from the ground and handed it to his mother as a piece of kindling for the fire.

2 Mademoiselle C.D., who in 1922 was diagnosed as having tuberculous peritonitis which had progressed over several years into generalised tuberculosis involving kidneys, lungs and various other organs. In 1941 she was taken to Lourdes and bathed in the baths, and on 6 October at 7 p.m. was found to be free from the disease. The cure was confirmed by eight doctors after numerous tests.

The records at the Bureau des Constatations contain scores of detailed healings confirmed by photographs, X-rays and all the paraphernalia that goes with laboratory tests. Each healing has been corroborated by numerous physicians and medical specialists. Indeed no healing miracle is recorded unless it is confirmed by stringent tests and examinations made by not one but several doctors. I have been to Lourdes four times and have studied some of these records and can vouch for their authenticity.

Undoubtedly these miraculous healings are facilitated by the good offices of Mary, the Mother of Jesus, using her motherly influence by interceding on our behalf. It should be remembered, though, that she herself does not in any way heal us; Jesus her Son does that. She pleads for us in the same way as she prevailed upon her Son to change the water into wine at the wedding in Cana (John 2:1–11).

In 1984 I was diagnosed as having cancer. I underwent surgery and a long course of radiotherapy. During this time, my wife, Joan, my family and many friends and relatives prayed for me. On several occasions I was prayed over and was anointed with oil as recommended in the epistle of St James (5:14). I was also bathed several times in the baths at Lourdes.

I believe that I have been healed of my cancer. For me this was not a spontaneous or dramatic healing. In fact, in the early days several alarming symptoms seemed to persist, but gradually these disappeared, and now with greater confidence I feel that I have been healed, and give thanks for the wonders of medical science and for the skill of my surgeon and oncologist. I am also eternally grateful for all the many prayers and healing sessions that were carried out on my behalf. My wife Joan has also had cancer and has had similar treatment and prayers. I believe that she too has been healed.

I will perhaps be excused for continuing with this personal narrative. I believe I also have what for me can only be called 'my thorn in the flesh', which takes the form of generalised arthritis. I have prayed about this and indeed have been prayed over and anointed with oil several times. Although there is much improvement in the condition, some discomfort still continues. Like many sufferers with this complaint, I notice that as I start each day my symptoms are at their worst. But by the time I have had my 'quiet' period, my symptoms have receded somewhat, and the arthritis has become tolerable. It is as if God has decided that I should retain this particular 'thorn', and that each day I should ask to be given the grace to bear with it. I have not given up the hope that one day my arthritis will be healed. For the present, this has the effect of teaching me my dependence upon God and on his son Jesus Christ. In the intimacy of my soul I am able to feel his grace and know that all is well. This intimate contemplative attitude helps me not only to deal with the nuisance of arthritis, but also gives me grace and guidance for each day. I am taking his yoke upon me, as Jesus asks of us in one of his agricultural metaphors (Matthew 11:29–30).

As the author of *The Cloud of Unknowing* says

What I am, Lord, I offer you, for it is yourself.

(Extract from 'The Epistle of Privy Counsel')

Bibliography

Biggs, Robert. Medicine in Ancient Mesopotamia. *History of Science*, **8/96**. London, Wellcome Institute. 1969

Black's Bible Dictionary. Ed. M. & J.L. Miller. London, A. & C. Black. 1959

Blue, Lionel. Source of the Garden of Eden. BBC broadcast, January. 1991

Borst, James M.H.M. *Contemplative Prayer*. Missouri, Liguori Publications. 1979

Bronowski, J. *The Ascent of Man*. London, BBC. 1973

Camp, John. *The Healer's Art*. London, Frederick Muller. 1978

Claxton, K.T. William Roentgen. Geneva, Edito-Service. 1970

The Cloud of Unknowing and Other Works. Author unknown. Penguin Books. 1978

Coleman, Vernon. *The Story of Medicine*. London, Robert Hale. 1985

Coleman, Vernon. Overstaffed, inefficient and greedy. *The Daily Mail*, June 1991

Daniels, Anthony. How can we minister to the British Disease. *The Daily Telegraph*, June 1991

Dawson, C.G. *Healing, Pagan and Christian*. London, S.P.C.K. 1935

Eaton, Theodore H. Jr. *Evolution*. University of Kansas and Nelson, London. 1970

Goldsmith, Maurice. *The Curie Family*. Geneva, Edito-Service. 1971

Good News Bible. Swindon, The Bible Societies. 1976

Grant, F.C. and Rowley, H.H. *Dictionary of the Bible.* Edinburgh, T. & T. Clark. 1973

Hamilton, Elizabeth. *The Great Teresa.* London, Universe Books. 1963

Hastings, J. *Dictionary of Christ and the Gospels.* Edinburgh, T. & T. Clark. 1933

Health of the Nation. Summary of Government Proposals – Consultative Document for Health in England. London, Department of Health. 1991

Heaton, E.W. *Everyday life in Old Testament times.* London, Batsford. 1956

Huggett, Joyce. *Listening to God.* London, Hodder & Stoughton. 1986

Leakey, Richard. *Man and Nature.* London, Aldus Books
— — *The Making of Mankind,* London, Michael Joseph. 1981

Mazak, Vratislav. *Prehistoric Man: The Dawn of our Species.* London, Hamlyn. 1980

McKenna, Briege, O.S.C. with Libersat, Henry. *Miracles do Happen.* Dublin, Veritas Publications. 1987

McNeill, W.H. *Plagues and Peoples.* Oxford, Blackwell. 1977

A New Catechism: The Catholic Faith for Adults. London, Search Press. 1969

Rhodes, Philip. *An Outline History of Medicine.* London, Butterworths. 1985

Ross-MacDonald, Malcolm. *Every Living Thing: Man and Nature,* part 1. London, Aldus Books. 1975

Weatherhead, L.D. *Psychology, Religion and Healing.* London, Hodder & Stoughton. 1968

The Word Amongst Us. Vol. 10, No. 9. Harlow, Essex. 1991